STRATEGIC
PLAY

STRATEGIC PLAY

THE CREATIVE FACILITATOR'S GUIDE VOLUME #11

STORIES FROM THE GLOBAL PLAYGROUND

WITH LEGO® SERIOUS PLAY® METHODS

Strategic Play ▷

www.strategicplay.com
hello@strategicplay.com

Jacqueline Lloyd Smith, MA, MBA, (CMC), (ATR), et el.

Strategic Play

www.strategicplay.com
hello@strategicplay.com

ISBN: 978-1-78324-226-9

A CIP catalogue record for this book is available from the British Library

Published by Wordzworth
www.wordzworth.com

Please note, all photographs were taken pre-COVID 19.

CONTENTS

DEDICATION

This book is for all the creative risk-takers around the world who have joined us on this journey of play and innovation. Also, we are all forever indebted to the LEGO® Systems Group for their hard work and dedication inventing this tool that has allowed us to find and forge our unique paths in this world powered by the most playful methods. And a big thank you to Andrea, whose amazing editing skills we put to the test on this global project.

FOREWORD

Dr. Steve Ralph

*Practitioner Faculty, Pepperdine Graziadio Business School;
Founder, EPIC Impact Society; CEO, Open Ingenuity, LLC,
Certified LEGO® SERIOUS PLAY® Facilitator*

In an age where organizations must navigate turbulent changes, it is imperative to stay innovative to survive. The volatile marketplace, the exponential growth of technology, pandemics, generational differences in the workplace, and other complex world events all contribute to organizational disruption on various levels. Finding the right methodologies and tools to facilitate employee engagement for organizational innovation is critical. While there are a variety of innovative tools and methodologies to consider applying, I have found LEGO® SERIOUS PLAY® (LSP) is one of the most unique available.

Utilizing a 3D thinking approach, LEGO Serious Play participants build their ideas using LEGO bricks, resulting in full participation during a playful learning experience where innovation can thrive. As someone who continually utilizes this methodology in universities, organizations, and community events, I have witnessed how LSP can break down various barriers, catalyze creativity, and facilitate engagement where other tools cannot. Applying LEGO Serious Play in teams provides an incredible opportunity for participants to engage in the creative problem-solving process, to tell stories, and to facilitate the psychological safety and trust needed to cultivate innovation.

As one of the first licensed partners with the LEGO Systems Group, Strategic Play Group founder, Jacqueline Lloyd Smith, has incredible depth and expertise in this methodology. I have found her ability to apply and design LEGO Serious Play programs across a multitude of industries very inspiring. In this book, Jacqueline and members of the Strategic Play Global training team share their perspectives and experiences using LEGO Serious Play within their respective cultures. Readers will find valuable insights and facilitation tips that highlight how versatile and impactful LSP can be, regardless of location.

I am pleased to see there is now a resource like this book, which will provide readers with a global tour of how other professionals have used and seen LEGO Serious Play crossing borders to encourage creativity, collaboration, and communication.

PREFACE

By Jacqueline Lloyd Smith, MA, MBA, (ATR), (CMC), (FRSA)
Founder: Strategic Play Global

Our team of creative thinkers is spread around the globe, working in varied cultures that each present their own unique challenges and opportunities. This book is a collection of our stories, which we wrote to reflect upon and highlight the diversity of our individual experiences applying LEGO® SERIOUS PLAY® methods in our various regions. It is our hope that in sharing our experiences, we can help others who are working in this field and strive for more creative approaches to problem-solving, engagement, team-building, branding, and innovation.

Before March 2020, when COVID-19 shut down our head office in Canada, our trainers in China and Australia had already alerted our team to the fact a pandemic was coming. As each of our global trainers reported more and more closings, we found comfort in our weekly calls. These helped us to stay connected, share experiences, and offer support.

It was during these meetings we realized the uniqueness of our situation and the incredible value of our connections. We are a group of friends brought together through our love of LSP methods, despite the fact we live in very different countries: Australia, Bolivia, Brazil, Canada, Germany, Hong Kong, Macau, Mexico, Nigeria, Panama, Spain, UK, and USA. We have come to realize that while we love the method for its amazing application and results, we all have moments where we hate the inherent challenge of dealing with adults who assume it is too childish to be a valuable tool. We each continue our work to overcome this barrier.

As a team, we decided the COVID-19 shutdowns that prevented us from running in-person trainings were handing us the perfect opportunity to tell our global story. We each set to work writing a chapter to address the following challenge: Find three major insights you have had while working in your respective country and culture that will give others a glimpse into your part of the world and how it impacts the willingness of people to try something new.

It is very difficult, of course, to write about a culture when you are yourself a part of it. To observe your own culture's peculiarities, you have to venture outside it to see how it compares with others. Because Strategic Play is a global organization, we often talk and think about how our experiences differ. We do not claim to be cultural experts. Rather, we have humbly written these stories to share our individual experiences and what it was like to introduce such a new and novel tool into the areas where we live and work.

If you are new to LEGO® SERIOUS PLAY® and there is a chapter on your country, you will want to make particular note of it. You may gain some insights into how to introduce this method in your own work or community. The writer's experiences may also help you to navigate obstacles and offer inspiration. If you have a general interest in learning about different cultures, you will gain insights into the role geography plays in influencing the willingness of people to accept and try new things.

When you read these stories, you feel a thread connecting us. For this reason, the stories are fun to read. They illustrate how we are all so very much alike as humans, no matter where we live.

1

DENMARK:
WHERE IT ALL BEGAN

By Jesper Just Jensen

I am going to share my insights from my personal journey working for the LEGO® Systems Group, dating back to 2005. I have watched the LEGO® SERIOUS PLAY® method grow into what it is now: a community movement. It is quite interesting to reflect on the amazing potential of this tool, and how it has grown from where it was to where it is now.

■■ THE EARLY DAYS: LSP WAS A LEAN START-UP INSIDE LEGO® ■■

My name is Jesper Just Jensen, and I worked for LEGO® from 2005 – 2014. At first, I was responsible for leading the division of LEGO® SERIOUS PLAY®. I was recruiting strategic partners from around the world to help get LSP methods into the board-rooms and classrooms, where we knew it could have a very interesting impact. Later, I worked on an internal strategy process that led to an opening for me to join LEGO® Education; I brought LSP for schools along with me. We reengineered the process a bit to make it fit into a classroom. We came up with Build to Express, which still had the LSP process behind it. But it was a tool for language arts.

It all began when I was working at Microsoft, around 2005, when I was con-tacted by an old friend. He wondered if I might be interested in a job at the LEGO® SYSTEMS GROUP, as Director of LEGO® SERIOUS PLAY®. At the time, there were only about 15 – 16 LSP facilitators around the world using this method; we called them licensed partners. I thought this sounded like a great opportunity. It sounded especially interesting when I heard the LEGO® Group, as a company, was also in serious financial trouble.

People asked why I would leave my job with Microsoft for a company that was going belly up. Everyone thought it was a stupid idea. But learning about the company's problems made the opportunity very exciting for me. I went through an executive interview process. I had four meetings, and one was with Kjeld Kirk Kristensen (the owner). I will talk more about the importance of his leadership later. But at the time, I was very surprised Kjeld would be interested in me or this very small division.

My first two years, we were actively building up the LSP business as a division of LEGO®. We were recruiting new licensed partners to sell the process and facili-tate inside companies, making sure they could serve as we needed them to by expanding the reach of this new tool. We also experimented with the LSP process, to use in the areas of family development and education. We realized it was a tool that is very good for strategy development. As we peeled back all the layers, we found it was and is very good for personal reflection and clearly communicating your ideas, views, and perspectives.

The essence of LSP is that it is a very strong and effective communication tool. But we saw that it could also be useful for other situations, where you want people to have effective dialogue about solving problems, ideas, managing conflicts, identifying missions, and things like that. We began by exploring it with family coaching. We did a lot of testing and prototyping with family counselors, and it turned out to be a very good method. Our test subjects really enjoyed using this approach.

LEGO® Education assisted with the development of the tool by helping to consider the methodology of thinking and learning. From a team perspective, we wanted to consider how people engage in a group. We were really considering things like:

- How do you best learn?
- How do you best engage through collaboration with others in teamwork?
- How do you ignite creative thinking and critical thinking into a process?
- How do you make sure everybody is heard?
- How do you make sure everybody listens to each other to value what others are saying, so they can build something even stronger together?

We realized things go wrong because people often do not listen to each other. They listen more to themselves and try to get their agendas through.

So that marriage of strategy thinking and organizational development thinking, and also the learning theory from LEGO® Education, was the early ignition of LSP. And so there are a lot of fundamental values of human belief in those frameworks. That is also what came out when we brought together this group of five or eight people.

We were contacted by schoolteachers who had tried LSP, and they said it would be a wonderful tool for school. So we began testing and getting closer to that audience, as well. It seemed the education route was a more viable and relevant business than family development. We already had an internal customer with the LEGO® Education company, which does educational tools for schools and after-school competitions. LSP was a natural product line that we could feed into LEGO® Education.

■■ THE EARLY CHALLENGES OF MOVING THIS METHOD OUT INTO THE BUSINESS WORLD VIA THE COMMUNITY OF PARTNERS ■■

We began looking for consultants with established and credible businesses and clients to partner with us. We called these early consultants LEGO® SERIOUS PLAY® Licensed Partners. And we needed these early adopters who were serious, because we were requiring five days of training to be certified in LSP. We spent time getting to know them, not just their qualifications but also their desires and motivation. When you start something like this, it is fragile in many ways. We did not want that to affect quality. Therefore, we were looking for credible and professional consultants to become licensed partners who could facilitate the process and add good brand equity to the LEGO® SERIOUS PLAY® division.

I got a lot of inquiries every day, and I spent a lot of time sorting through them to see who was serious and who was not. And then with the people who were serious, it was a matter of taking them to where they would keep going and really make a business out of this application. There was the certification training and the license payment, which I guess for consultants was not insignificant. The yearly license was around EUR 5,000. I needed to make sure the potential licensed partner understood they would be looking at a EUR 10,000 upfront commitment to get started.

Because of this significant investment, the hard sell was important. From the experience we had with our testing partners, when they had been training or when customers tried LSP, we knew it was worth it. There was no doubt. The hard sell was actually to get the end user to understand the value of LEGO® SERIOUS PLAY® and what the outcome would be. Once trained, these licensed partners really had to use their full passion and persuasiveness to convince potential customers about the value of LSP so they would try it.

This was a tough sell for them, of course. It was a different time. People were not as open to using toys or play in a business context. Of course, you could say when you are getting in for EUR 10,000 it is not about a toy. They are bricks used for play with kids, but the hands-on, mind-engaged "constructionistic" way you put the bricks together is what creates the benefits of LSP. You have a model, a transitional object, or an artifact for conversation or reflection, where you can externalize your thoughts or what you are talking about. When you have had it in your hands and you start to realize and see the power of how it can help you reflect and communicate about the topic, even a complex topic, that is when people start to see the power of the LEGO® build as a transitional object rather than a toy.

I liked the idea of getting LSP into the hands of anybody, wherever they were on the globe. So we were not very restrictive about geography. Of course we took it into account, but anybody could meet the criteria and join. We wanted this licensed partner community to grow fast, so in the beginning we did not want too many people in the same country and same region.

It is a funny paradox. This LSP tool is really your competitive differentiator, but you are hindered if you use it upfront in your marketing communications. It is a bit of a funny dilemma. We were really pulling the hair out of our heads to find a way to communicate and market this. Everyone, the licensed partners and those of us at LEGO®, understood it was really hard to sell this process tool upfront. We tried different things, but it was a difficult time to sell this. But what was really good to see was the passion and consistent perseverance of keeping this, because at LEGO® we used it internally and could see the value of it.

THE IMPORTANCE OF LEADERSHIP FROM KJELD KIRK KRISTENSEN (LEGO®'S OWNER) AND THE LICENSED PARTNER COMMUNITY (THE EARLY ADOPTERS)

The founder of the LEGO® Systems Group was the CEO and third generation owner, Kjeld. In the beginning, Kjeld was one of the incubators of this whole idea. During LEGO® 's tough period in the 2000s, the senior team brought in outside consultants

to help find a new direction for the company. And what Kjeld realized, was often the answer to some of the problems was not necessarily coming from one of the outside consultants. They were coming from people who were already in the company. He quickly realized this and began working with two professors from Institute for Management Development (IMD). One was a strategy professor, and the other was an organizational development professor. Kjeld wanted an answer to this question: How might we embolden our own people in the problem-solving of the company? Because we need to hear from them. That was the fundamental belief. And how can we use LEGO® bricks to uncover the answers that lie within our people?

Kjeld believed in this process from the beginning. As it matured he was also on my advisory board, keeping his visible hand over this and the high price of LEGO®. There were plenty of opportunities and reasons to kill it along the way, but the power of what LSP could do for those who got it in their hands and heads was just so powerful. We saw this in the business area, but also when we got it into the hands of teachers and kids. We saw what a difference it made to create a path to change for kids. It helped children who maybe had a hard time communicating their ideas, their thoughts, their fears. This gave them another tool they had not had before. We saw teachers in tears, because before they had not been able to get through to those kids. And now they had a new method to do that.

So we all viewed LSP as very powerful. And as the new licensed partners went through the training, from Monday to Friday, there was a big aha moment. They understood from the beginning it was a very powerful process. But during the week, they saw many more possibilities as they tried it out in their own hands. And that just gave us a very strong and powerful partner community that was doing everything to try to get it in the hands of more people, even though it was hard at the time. But there were also plenty of opportunities for the partners to leave and just do something else. And this is also why the concept is still alive today. Even though LEGO® has kind of left it to the community to grow on their own, the original licensed partners are the ones who stood by it and kept it going because they believed in the process.

We did internal conferences in the learning days. We brought together the partners, even though they were coming from all parts of the world: Japan, South America,

Canada, and South Africa. In the early days, people were coming in to meet up with soulmates and fellow minds to share. You could say we were kind of a lean start-up at that point. We were small. We were trying to grow. We were trying to build something and try it out and see what worked and what did not work and changed directions.

So in many ways, you could say we were also all joining a community effort of a new business start-up. And that has not only matured, but you could say we got a lot of interesting learning along the way. One was the conferences that were set up. We knew if we could get in front of maybe 100 people, and do a small activity with LSP, maybe from 15 minutes to an hour long, we knew after we left we would get at least two or three serious leads. That led to something else, and then led to three other leads. So it was a slow process in the beginning, but it grew gradually from there.

You can look at the resistance we heard from all angles. So many things were internal in the company. LEGO® started in a good place. And everywhere I got, whether it was supply chain or other places, people would ask, "Why are we doing this? Why didn't we kill it off?" But we kept on, because we had a guy like Kjeld on the board. And he had a bigger thought and vision for this. He saw LEGO® as more than just a toy for play, but also as a universal communication tool. It was very important to Kjeld, as well as other key executives at LEGO®, to support this, despite the fact we should probably have focused on other things and spent resources on other things.

The same goes with the licensed partners. They also saw a lot of resistance in the beginning. But I am glad everybody listened to them and did not listen to all the voices that said, "This is a bad idea. Don't do this." LSP is not like other products that have a huge, positive receptors. Most products at LEGO® typically get bought and they take off. But this did not take off by itself. It was quite a lot of hard work from everybody.

There are a lot of pitfalls in the communication process that LSP was looking to eliminate, and has done so very nicely. That was also based on a fundamental belief in people, and maybe from a Scandinavian niche part of the order from Kjeld. He followed this all the way from the beginning and supported and put his heart and will behind making this something LEGO® would put into more hands in the world.

Kjeld was always part of the advisory board in the beginning, supporting the development of some of the other areas. But he would gladly join in the learning days with the partners. He would put in a few words into the meet and greet with the partners, showing his belief and passion in it as well. This despite the fact LSP was of course only a small fraction of LEGO® when seen from the size perspective. But from an impact perspective, Kjeld saw it as equal and so he followed that along the way.

And then it grew around bringing different community stakeholders together. In the learning days, these were the licensed partner meetings we had one or two years. This ignited another idea for the LEGO® Idea Conference. We wanted to make a bigger impact, to see if we can gravitate people around the idea of play, learning, and creativity for both kids and adults. The first year we did the LEGO® Idea Conference, up to half the participants were coming from the LSP licensed partner community. The strong support for that made it grow from a small conference into something that became really big over the years.

It shows the power of the community. If LSP had not been supported by the licensed community spirit, if it was just consultants that took the tool and went on their own, it would not have gotten to what it is today. The community was rallying around this, coming together, and building it together, even though many of them were also in many ways competitors. It was the same thing with the LEGO®

Idea Conference. It grew into something bigger because people were coming together around a common purpose. The same goes with LEGO®, as well. There is the whole adult playing community making more engagement around this. So it shows it is not just about a tool and the product. It is about people building a community around this that is still alive today.

I think the fact this keeps growing, despite the challenges it has faced, shows the power of the LSP community. Maybe even think of it as a society. You create a society of people that are either receiving the benefits of the experience or delivering. And a society has a lot of variations. There are a lot of cultures. And I think about the fact that the basic idea with LSP is around reflection and communication. That a basic idea can be, with your own imagination, applied in so many different ways to so many different problems. I really believe with the community of users and practitioners they will bring it in to make even more use cases.

THE FUTURE FOR LSP

How many people have been to an LSP workshop? There must be thousands and thousands of people by now. I can even guess 50,000 people. And when 50,000 people have an immersive experience like this, these are memories for life. They will be asking for it, getting back to it at some point in time. I think we are over that critical point of people that have had the experience, and they will come back and ask for it. It is just like LEGO®, just on a different scale. So many parents grew up with LEGO®. And that is also a key at LEGO®, to keep them growing and growing. There are so many parents that have a passion for LEGO® that they're bringing to their kids as well.

And you could say in the same way, just in a small scale, there are now so many people that have LSP in their hearts and minds that it keeps going. I would expect it to grow and I would expect to see a lot of the creative consultants using this for many more purposes than we thought about in the beginning. We started with strategy development, team development, and personal development, but the imagination has grown this into so many different categories and problems. It is only the imagination that limits how you can use it, when you think of it as a reflection and communication tool. I think they really appreciate this is something that has a life of its own. The LEGO® Systems Group also appreciates the fact that LEGO® is so much more than boxes of police stations and Star Wars. It is something where the community has taken it in so many other directions than the LEGO® company could think of.

I use LSP every day, without using the bricks even. An old colleague used to say, "It's just about getting into LSP mode." You have done it so many times and you also value the knowns and the values behind the thinking, how you want to engage people in dialogue. You want to make sure everybody's heard, even the lonely guy, as is the metaphor. I use it every day in terms of effective communication and problem-solving and follow the LSP ground rules. Of course, it is more effective when used in the disciplined process and you have the bricks and the right questions. But it is so powerful, it gives you a certain mindset you can use in your daily life in every meeting.

There is something about creating new meaning when you are building and talking about your build. You are thinking and creating new meaning. You are learning new things. You are also learning new things from the dialogue you have with your peers, in a nonintrusive and openminded way. You are learning new things about yourself and others, and this is how it brings you to a new place. I think that is also very powerful, why people are getting so engaged and can see so much value in what they have built. It is hard to imagine where this will go, other than it will just keep growing as more and more people experience the power of this method.

2

AFRICA:
A CREATIVE AND YOUTH-FULL CONTINENT

"Ignite passion

to fuel innovation"

By Daberechi Okedurum

"When pushed to the wall, there is only one choice to make; in Africa, we choose creativity."

—DABERECHI OKEDURUM

Africa is seen as the last frontier, rich in so many natural resources. It is also known as the continent with the largest number of young people in the world. How does creativity thrive here? How is the older generation getting on with the realities of the Fourth Industrial Revolution and the demand for new thinking on how we work and do business? And finally, how are people using LEGO® SERIOUS PLAY® methods to help ensure we have an equipped young population that can transform Africa into a first-world nation? We will be finding answers to the above questions in this chapter. And in the end, I hope you find a compass fit enough to get you ready to sail across Africa on your creative quest.

I am a certified creative problem-solving practitioner and a certified LSP facilitator and licensed trainer. I am an experiential learning enthusiast, leading facilitations within and outside Africa. I have even been a spotlight speaker at the prestigious annual Creative Problem Solving Institute (CPSI) in Buffalo, New York—the largest gathering of creativity practitioners in the world. My work takes me to board-rooms with top management teams, to the workstations of entrepreneurs, and to institutions of learning. My commitment is borne out of the need to develop creative thinking capacities of individuals, organizations, and institutions, helping them apply their creative behaviors to building valuable products, processes, or services.

I became fascinated by LSP during CPSI at the University at Buffalo in 2015, where I was attending as one of the pioneer Sidney Parnes Global Fellows. I opted for the LSP introduction course and became hooked; I also made a good connection with my now longtime friend Dr. Steve Ralph, also a licensed trainer. Interestingly, Dr. Steve and Jacquie introduced me to and connected me with two Strategic Play licensed trainers in Nigeria: April Anazodo and Dr. Jumoke Fola-Alade, an amazing duo I have been working with for over three years now in the African region.

UNDERSTANDING CREATIVITY IN AFRICA

Africa has grown in its creativity. From experience, I have seen how Africans are maintaining a high level of creativity despite being in a society enormously lack-ing in resources. So I will be highlighting some of the key sectors like Technology (ICT), agriculture, healthcare, and how deliberate creativity and innovation is being used to transform these industries. I will be painting a before and after picture of the sectors, from years ago to what they are today. This section explains what we know about creativity in Africa, from my experience of working here. It also shows how anyone who is interested in contributing to creativity in Africa can take advantage of the local business intelligence, including the external factors limit-ing the practice of creativity.

Considering the widely held view that Africa is a struggling continent with enor-mous hardships and a lack of resources, one might assume we are not abreast with the realities of the Fourth Industrial Revolution. We are actually very engaged in deliberate creativity and innovation. Just as every nation on earth has its struggles, the challenges in Africa are breeding a unique level of creativity and innovation. We are witnessing the gradual rise of superpowers, which shines a light on political instability, employment rates, and the increasing inequality of income and resources. These differences highlight the need to create solutions that meet the needs of local communities and enable them to compete in regional and global markets.

Two decades ago, as a boarding school student in my mother's village in Southeastern Nigeria, it was difficult for our parents or relatives to send us money from the city. Ours was like many rural communities across Africa, with a large unbanked population. However, before my graduation we took advantage of the advent of mobile phones with a simple solution: Receiving digits of call vouchers through text/SMS, and reselling them to nearby mobile phone call centers in exchange for cash. This single solution has been advanced in several towns; and today, Africa has one of the finest mobile money transfer solutions in the world. This helps many living in rural unbanked areas and cities to send and receive money with ease.

For many years, agriculture in Africa was seen as a social program funded by aids from international development organizations and advanced economies, such as the United States and the United Kingdom, to support poor rural farmers and promote food sustainability. In 2016, Nigeria witnessed the birth of its first digital agriculture investment platform that enables Nigerians, or investors anywhere in the world, to invest in improving the activities and livelihood of rural farmers from the comfort of their homes. These farmers no longer depend on international aid, and more individuals have been inspired to venture into agriculture as a business. The young team of inventors did not allow lack of resources to stand in their way. They insisted on asking questions, making connections, and finding resources to impact millions of lives across the continent.

The above examples are just a fraction of the entrepreneurial and creative spirit flowing across Africa. At age 11, Richard Turere of Kenya invented a flashlight system powered by solar energy to save cows from being attacked in their pens by lions. In turn, this saved thousands of lions from being killed by herders. [1] At 14, William Kamkwamba used spare bicycle parts and scraps to build a windmill for his rural village in Malawi.[2] West Africa's first air ambulance service was started by a young Dr. Ola Orekunrin, who was inspired to venture into seemingly impossible terrain following the death of her 12-year-old sister.[3] The list of inspiring stories is endless.

Difficult challenges and a lack of resources are a trigger for creativity and innovation in Africa, but they can also trigger crime and violence. It solely depends on the lens from which you view the continent. The conditions motivate people to keep asking questions, looking for available resources within and reaching out

---

[1]   *Richard Turere*. Anzisha Prize. (n.d.). *https://anzishaprize.org/fellows/richard-turere/*.

[2]   Kamkwamba, W. (n.d.). *William Kamkwamba*. TED. *https://www.ted.com/speakers/william_kamkwamba*.

[3]   Posted by: Karen Frances Eng August 3, & Eng, K. F. (n.d.). *The flying doctor: Fellows Friday with Ola Orekunrin*. TED Blog. https://blog.ted.com/the-flying-doctor-fellows-friday-with-ola-orekunrun/.

to the community to leverage on the strengths of others. With so many weak government institutions, unstable policies and currency in so many states and its resulting impact on business, foreign investors see the continent as a high-risk environment. However, Africa delivers one of the highest returns on investments following population size and level of competition. Despite the obvious challenges, indigenous businesses have learned to flow with the tide and not adhere strictly to the books, making deliberate creativity a necessity for survival.

No doubt, Africa is a creative continent. For over 24 years, the likes of Kobus Neethling Institute have been shaping the creative behaviors of business leaders—and educators, most recently— in Africa[4]. Our experience here does not leave us in doubt about the impact of creative-thinking problem-solving tools and methodology in Africa. These are being used to make abstract ideas concrete, ideas inspired by the needs and challenges facing millions of Africans. The

---

[4] "Home – The Kobus Neethling Institute Beyonder Training Programme," The Kobus Neethling Institute, April 20, 2021, http://www.kninstitute.com/.

potentials of a deliberate creative-thinking, problem-solving, and communicating tool and methodology cannot be overemphasized. It comes in handy to help open the eyes of Africans to see the vast amount of natural and human resources in and around them. It pushes them in their quest to find answers, make connections, and create groundbreaking products, services, and processes that serve their communities and, by extension, the global market.

REKINDLING THE CREATIVE CAPACITY OF AFRICA'S BABY BOOMERS AND GEN X; THE STRUGGLES AND THE WINS

One of the biggest challenges in this field is working with baby boomers and Generation X. Interestingly, this demographic controls a majority of organizations in Africa because they comprise the top management teams and are decision-makers. So here I present my experience working with this age group. I will go from convincing them to accept a new way of thinking that involves the use of LEGO® to having them show up for workshops, as well as the feedback I receive on their views of LSP's impact. I also present the generational differences I have identified in the workplace and how each reacts to activities, processes, and sessions on creativity and LSP tools.

In most African countries, a large number of businesses operate in the informal sector. Many of these businesses are not registered with the government authorities and do not function with the typical business structure found in business management textbooks. While many training organizations like ours are still working towards a creative method to engage and build business skills in the informal sector (most cannot afford existing training fees), there is a jostle by local and international professional training and development firms for businesses in the real/formal sector such as banks, FMCGs (fast moving consumer goods), telecom firms, oil and gas, and several multinationals who often earmark budgets for staff training and development.

There are several challenges that limit the possibility of securing a creative thinking and communication workshop for these organizations; for most of them, especially the multinational firms, the standard operating procedure, strategy, and creativity that run the entire organization is developed at their global head office in Europe or North America. This makes the local extension here a mere center for execution with little or no room to take on initiatives from scratch. When training is needed, top management staff are invited to the global office. This reality limits the number of businesses available to reach out to in the formal sector.

Another challenge we encountered working with the formal sector is that a good number of the businesses run on a tall structure, with bureaucratic processes that takes months to bid and secure a contract. We identified this was the case in most firms where the majority of decision-makers were comprised of baby boomers and Gen Xers; technology firms had more decision-makers under the age of 45 than their counterparts in traditional establishments. Our success in working with firms having both baby boomers and Gen X is borne out of the need to fulfil the desires and convictions of the younger generations of the decision-making team. They believe training/consulting in creative thinking and communication with LSP will positively impact their productivity and, by extension, improve the profit margin of the organization. This category of decision-makers sees play as an integral part of their work and a good way to communicate and engage younger members of the workforce to achieve organizational goals; globalization has kept them abreast with current methods and processes used by organizations around the world.

Interestingly, for organizations bold enough to work with us, we have never received negative feedback from baby boomers or Generation X. We get testimonials such as this one, from a participant over the age of 60, "At first, seeing your LEGO, I felt like I was being invited for a child's play, out of my busy schedule, and hoped our investment for your training was worth it. But now I can tell that these tools are highly engaging, encourages deeper and richer conversation with my team and it has helped us make the connections we need to grow our business."

One training at a time, we have been able to show a range of groups, from university academics to top management teams, that LSP is a great tool for the fast and dynamic nature of today's business environment. While it is still a challenge to initiate the conversation and convince baby boomers and Gen X managers to get their organizations on board, through the testimonial and word-of-mouth of successful trainees, we see a good number coming on board to mix up with the younger generation who are most excited about LSP.

▬ SOLVING ONE PROBLEM AT A TIME: CONTRIBUTION OF LSP IN BUILDING SKILLS OF AFRICA'S YOUNG POPULATION ▬

Africa has the largest number of young people compared to any other continent in the world. Here is where the youth-full part of the chapter comes in. The challenge before many organizations, institutions, and even governments is equipping this young population with the right skills to make them meaningful members of society. Our contribution is using LSP as a powerful tool to develop skills needed in the workplace, as well as to build sustainable ventures and to succeed in life in general. The biggest asset for Africa right now is her young population, and LSP is making a meaningful contribution to how they acquire knowledge and skills. It is an approach worth scaling, and I intend to make that case here.

For us, Africa's biggest asset is her people and most importantly the young populace. As an organization, one of our core purposes is to equip these young minds to transform Africa into a first-world nation. They will lead the next level of creativity and innovation and become meaningful contributors to the continent and beyond with the appropriate creative-thinking, problem-solving, and communication skills that empower their curiosity and knowledge they gained in school. This will drastically reduce the scourge of unemployment and youth restiveness on the continent.

Fortunately, we have worked with organizations and institutions committed to training young people. We have lead sessions at Leap Africa's Social Innovators Programme & Awards (SIPA), an accelerator fellowship that empowers young changemakers to deliver more impact and build sustainable social enterprises that offer effective solutions to challenges in local communities across Nigeria.[5] With LSP, these young minds were able to connect and effectively communicate and prototype abstract social impact driven ideas for their respective communities.

Our session in Ghana, with the Meltwater Entrepreneurial School of Technology (MEST), enabled technology startups comprising teams from different African

---

5   "Sipa," LEAP Africa, accessed July 6, 2021, https://leapafrica.org/sipa/.

countries to apply LSP in asking deeper questions about their business ideas and strategies. This helped them to discover gray areas and gain clarity on their roles, as well as to effectively pitch to the school faculty and investors. MEST is an Africa-wide technology entrepreneur training program, internal seed fund, and network of hubs offering incubation for technology startups in Africa.[6]

Following our work with OPL Academy in Lagos, Nigeria, through their Tradesman Empowerment Program, we have been committed to using LSP in training high-potential tradesmen to develop competency in creative thinking, problem-solving, communication, and innovation. At the end, they are linked to full-time job placements, contracts, or apprenticeships. For this set of participants, it is amazing to see them think creatively with their hands using the LSP tools while developing global best practices. OPL Academy is an employment accelerator providing practical and scalable solutions to meet the talent demands of Nigeria's construction industry.[7]

The impact of a problem-based learning or experiential learning methodology for young people developing skills is enormous, but it is difficult to find institutions of higher learning that apply such methodologies. Most of these institutions have overcrowded classes and lack the requisite facilities and human resources to drive this kind of learning; therefore, students cannot make connections with the real world using knowledge they gain in the classroom. This reality contributes to the high rate of unemployable graduates in Africa. LSP stands a good chance in filling this hole in our educational system, given its proven success story in engaging the human senses of touch, sight, and sound. Illustrations with LSP tools make knowledge and ideas come to life in the form of something students can see, hear, and touch. From the classrooms of higher institutions to the training rooms of startup entrepreneurs, tradesmen, and career professionals, LSP activities and tools continues to show that indeed the mind is a goldmine.

CONCLUSION

The importance of a deliberate creative-thinking problem-solving and communication tool and methodology like LSP cannot be overemphasized. It opens the eyes of Africans to the vast amount of natural and human resources within and around them, and it pushes them in their quest to find answers, make connections, and create groundbreaking products, services, and processes that serves the community and by extension the global market.

---

[6] "MEST," MEST, accessed July 6, 2021, http://www.meltwater.org/.

[7] *Home*. OPL Academy. (n.d.). http://www.oplacademy.org/.

While it is still a challenge to initiate the conversation and convince baby boomers and Gen X top managers to get on board with the LSP methodology, we are gradually winning through testimonials and the word-of-mouth of successful trainees. Hopefully, in the nearest future, a good number will come on board to mix up with the younger generations who are most excited about LSP. Finally, LSP activities and tools continue to show that the goldmine in the mind of young Africans can be drilled and refined to help them transform Africa by connecting their abstractions and making them concrete.

3

BRAZIL: A CULTURE IN LOVE WITH BUILDING CONNECTIONS

By Kari Campos

Paulo Costa, and Ivonne Velasco Carreño

Ahh… Brazil! Those who either live in or have visited Brazil have experienced first-hand the warmth, the fun-loving spirit, and the unbelievable talent and creativity of the Brazilian people. They have heard the music that speaks to your soul, tasted the delicious food, gazed in awe at the breathtaking natural beauty, and admired the pride and preservation of a diversity of cultures. In Brazil, there are innumerable things to see, enjoy, and be inspired by.

While less evident to those who live outside Brazil's borders, it is worthy to note and study the drive, creativity, and resilience of the Brazilian people. Individuals, teams, and organizations thrive in a complex socio-political environment. The consequent dynamics in legislation, high tax rates, and overwhelmingly bureaucratic processes can inhibit agility when the fast-moving global economy requires it most. Yet the people of Brazil persevere, which is nothing short of a wonder of the world all in its own.

As a team, we reflected on our contribution to this book. We realized we have each seen LEGO® SERIOUS PLAY® consistently fast-track a variety of elements that are essential to sustainable success in a way that only this brain friendly, hands-on, play-based tool can. So where do we begin?

We were inspired by a popular saying in Brazil: By grain and grain, the hen fills its belly. We decided to use this opportunity to share a few granular glimpses into how we, as trainers and facilitators, have experienced success due to the interplay of Brazilian culture and LEGO® SERIOUS PLAY® methods. Further inspired by the wisdom of the LEGO® SERIOUS PLAY® methodology, we will begin with the individual and build our way up to teams and organizations.

■ LEGO® SERIOUS PLAY® AND THE INDIVIDUAL IN BRAZIL ■

Using LSP with an individual, or in a coaching or therapy session, can be very effective. It enhances both the elaboration of and reflection upon personal stories in a way that allows for broadening perspectives, insights, healing, growth, and development. The methodology has proven helpful time and again in sharing and exploring life experiences. This helps participants to speak directly and concretely about events, thoughts, and feelings. It also helps them to examine and evaluate, from different perspectives, the information they expressed through their 3D LEGO® models. This aspect of the method is true around the globe. Therefore, we will specifically look at how LSP relates to our experiences in working with individual team and organizational leaders in Brazil.

For many working professionals in Brazil, it is a dream job to become a manager or to take on a leadership position. Like many who take on such positions elsewhere, they are expected to control processes and projects, enhance motivation and engagement, and to understand the specific technical aspects of the work under their supervision. But compared to similar positions in other countries of South America, the salaries for management positions are higher in Brazil. They also include benefits such as a private office with a window, a covered parking space close to the entrance of the building, an administrative assistant to help stay on top of personal and professional tasks, and sometimes even a private driver. Such perks make these positions extremely desirable, and those who occupy them gain status and respect.

In our experience as LEGO® SERIOUS PLAY® facilitators, there is one aspect of Brazilian culture we feel really makes leaderships positions unique in our country. In David Livermore's book, *Expand Your Borders*[8], he describes the cultural value dimension of *power distance*. It shapes the way people interact. When power distance is low, social interactions are freer and people are generally more empowered to make decisions. But when the power distance is high, such as is the case in Latin America and consequently Brazil, status differences can restrict interactions among people and play a big part in who has decision-making authority.

We have found the perceived benefits and status of a leadership position must be properly managed, otherwise the leader may experience isolation in the workplace. This prevents the leader from establishing the kind of relationships with team members that allow for direct, honest, agile, and free-flowing exchanges. This type of communication is often necessary to effectively and efficiently address dynamic, pressing, and/or complex environments and issues.

A leader who desires a good communication flow with their team must address and manage the high power distance value in a way that serves the leader's intentions. Otherwise, overall results may suffer due to the leader's missing out on many of the team's thoughts and ideas. The leader might be left out of conversations team members are having around the water cooler or coffee station. Some team members may not feel comfortable approaching the leader to share their ideas on ways to improve a process, product, or project.

While facilitating sessions with leaders and teams in Brazil, we have seen how LEGO® SERIOUS PLAY® methods can quickly break down communication barriers and minimize the perceived power distance between leaders and team members. This happens because LSP creates a safe environment, builds trust, and offers team members and their leader a level playing field to openly share their thoughts and ideas about the topic they are discussing. Whether it be process improvement, product design, or team building, we have seen LSP's benefits both during and after sessions. We have seen teams build trust and then develop powerful solutions through the diversity of thought that naturally occurs when a team and its leaders have an open and trusting relationship.

---

[8]   Livermore, David, A. (2013), *Expand Your Borderers: discover ten cultural clusters*. East Lansing. Cultural Intelligence Center.

▬ BUILDING PERSONAL CONNECTIONS IN BRAZIL ▬

A variety of cultures have a significant economic and social impact in the country, including the Native Indigenous Brazilian, Portuguese, Spanish, Dutch, French, African, Arab, Japanese, and Italian. There is a palpable pride in Brazil's regional diversity, which is often so stark one can usually tell exactly where they are in the country based on architecture, accents, traditions, festivities, social practices, and even culinary dishes. Regardless of a region's dominant cultural influence, most Brazilians have a common desire to build relationships and connect with others.

Brazilians place a high value on their relationships, both personal and professional. The beginning of any meeting in Brazil, whether it be with a new potential business partner or a close colleague, conversation begins at a personal level. People share details about their personal lives and ask heartfelt questions of others. These conversations can include everything from favorite sports teams to the health of family members. The genuine interest in personal conversation is often the center of social and professional gatherings.

Conversation can be so central to business relationships, the time spent connecting over an espresso before a meeting can be just as important as time spent on the meeting's agenda. It is almost an unspoken rule in Brazil: First, we connect; then we work. Outsiders may be eager to get down to business on time, but this cultural habit of investing time in personal conversations can be very beneficial to teams and their organizations as a whole. Forging personal connections through stories of family, life, and work provides the opportunity to build trusting relationships. This can translate into higher engagement, productivity, effectiveness, and satisfaction in the workplace.

There is no right or wrong way to connect with others. But if you know people value relationships and enjoy connecting on a personal level, you also know developing connections is a big part of building trust among team members. Taking the time to do this can create high-performing teams. Sometimes organizations are interested in maximizing opportunities for their teams to build personal connections, rather than leaving it to happen organically or by chance. Cue LEGO® SERIOUS PLAY® methods.

Through the LSP process, we systematically provide an opportunity for everyone to reflect, open up, and cultivate insights. We allow them to expand their understanding of themselves and others, including the group as a whole. Through this expansion and clarity building, participants are able to connect effectively and personally while engaging at the group level.

We cannot control how much each person gives to relationship building, but we know from experience you cannot fabricate trust among team members. As Strategic Play® certified LEGO® SERIOUS PLAY® methods facilitators, we are trained to use this tool to maximize clarity on an individual and team level within a restricted time frame. Doing so helps to catalyze the outcome of time dedicated to the relationship building aspect of team development. Interestingly, while applying LEGO® SERIOUS PLAY® in Brazil, we have witnessed connections quickly become more concrete and inclusive as the participants easily build relationships while sharing their 3D models.

We have seen LEGO® SERIOUS PLAY® lead to amazing results. The method capitalizes on the fact most Brazilians innately enjoy being playful and building personal relationships in professional settings. It also provides a framework to have fun and connect with others systematically and collectively. Building these connections through play creates the fun and energetic environment Brazilians seem to thrive in. This helps to build momentum and contributes to building strong teams.

▬ CATALYZING CONVERSATIONS, INSIGHTS, AND ALIGNMENT OF TEAMS ▬

One interesting aspect of Brazilian culture is the flow of communication. Brazilians are passionate and fun loving, and in conversation they are eager to point out connections and share ideas with friends and colleagues. It is common for people to interrupt each other. They do this when they disagree but also when they want to offer support, make a joke, or share why they agree or identify with something someone else is saying. When somebody has an opinion or wants to make a comment about how the idea or experience relates to them, it is commonplace for them to get excited and passionately jump into the conversation. It is not seen as being rude or disrespectful. It is simply how conversations tend to flow in Brazil. This dynamic naturally increases the length of conversations, because people bounce freely between subjects and do not always bring closure to their initial topic.

Another interesting aspect of communication dynamics is the reluctance to say the word *no* to someone with whom the speaker is trying to develop or maintain a relationship. Socially and in business, it is rare to hear a direct *no*. If someone wants to turn something down, they will often do it in such a vague and roundabout way their response ends up leaving the listener unsure of the next steps.

Being dynamically participative and passionate in conversations, freely jumping from subject to subject, and withholding the word *no* all seem to nurture the value of developing and preserving authentic personal relationships. We do feel the Brazilian style of conversation is perfect over dinner and drinks with family, friends, and colleagues. But in the workplace, these cultural habits can be counterproductive.

In meetings, conversations can easily veer off topic. Depending on the power dynamics of those in the room, some people may dominate conversations meant to involve the entire team. This prevents some people from getting the opportunity to share their own ideas and opinions before the meeting ends. Meetings can run longer than expected or even be called to an end before addressing the most critical items on the agenda. Conversations requiring a yes or no answer can be limited to friendly chitchat and indirect responses, leaving people to make their own interpretations. In the business world, this translates to misunderstandings and the potential for wasted time and money.

These situations present potential bottlenecks in productivity. They can also have other negative impacts. Business culture, problem solving, decision-making processes, and overall forward movement of teams and organizations may suffer.

The ground rules and systematic process of LEGO® SERIOUS PLAY® determines that everyone shares their perspectives and ideas in turn, within a predetermined time frame and with limited resources. As participants work alone, using their hands to reflect and build models representing their thoughts, they activate different areas of the brain. Participants build with the LEGO® bricks to create three-dimensional artifacts representing their ideas. These models then serve as a visual aid as they share the details of their thoughts with the group. The facilitator holds space for each participant to share their perspective before allowing others to ask clarifying questions. This not only allows the speaker to finish their train of thought before others start injecting questions and comments, but it also allows for generous listening. Everyone knows they will get the same chance to fully share their views with the group.

This structured process naturally helps to keep conversations on track. It also catalyzes the possibility of generating new insights by allowing for the exposure and discussion of a wider range of perspectives in a shorter amount of time. Participants get to think deeper, make their points concisely, and provide more clarity to the group.

Strategic Play® trainers often use the term *hard fun*. We have learned LEGO® SERIOUS PLAY® methods help conversations and reflection to reach a new depth. The process helps to bring differences in perspectives, ideas, and even values to the forefront in a way that does not happen in conventional conversation alone. Some subjects are just too difficult or uncomfortable to pinpoint or address without the assistance of such an innovative tool.

Underlying issues that are not identified or addressed can easily block a team from moving forward. As facilitators, we have learned to commit to doing the groundwork and following the process of LSP. By doing so, we can help our participants see diversity of thought in a way that is fun, light, and productive. The process creates shared knowledge and practical insights people enjoy reflecting back on and applying over time. The alternative is to become weighed down by difficult and drawn-out conversations people cannot wait to forget.

It is important to note that while facilitators can use LEGO® SERIOUS PLAY® to unlock the information, knowledge, and creativity of the participants, we cannot try to control or force an outcome. The workshop results truly belongs to the participants. Unforeseen issues may arise as conversations go deeper, but we are confident these are an important part of what the participants needs to address to move forward and that LSP is one of the most productive ways to do it.

We have used LEGO® SERIOUS PLAY® methods to ease participants through seemingly complicated and sensitive subjects in a lighthearted and fun way. In a matter of hours, we help participants gain clarity and confidence. This helps them to define what, how, when, and why they should do something they have been indecisive about for a long period of time.

■■■ LEGO® SERIOUS PLAY® WITH ORGANIZATIONS IN BRAZIL ■■■

We would like to share the final grain of our experiences in Brazil by looking at the impact of LEGO® SERIOUS PLAY® at the organizational level. In the worlds of leadership and innovation, VUCA (Volatile, Uncertain, Complex, Ambiguous) is a word that describes turbulent environments. We feel companies aiming to succeed in Brazil must be prepared to embrace the realities of a VUCA atmosphere, perhaps even more so than their peers in other regions of the world. Just as diamonds are formed under pressure, the country's VUCA environment has contributed to cultivating a unique determination, resiliency, and creativity in Brazilians. Many working professionals here have impressive crisis-solving skills.

It is perhaps more difficult to find professionals who possess vision and experience in long-term planning. This is understandable considering how past economic events, such as nationwide double-digit inflation, have shown that long-term strategic planning can show a loss in terms of return on investment. So how do you get genius crisis-solvers to work together on teams and then get those teams comfortable with committing to long-term strategic planning?

LEGO® SERIOUS PLAY® helps harness the drive, resiliency, and creativity of individuals in a way that allows them to quickly share and understand ideas, develop and test prototypes in group settings, and ultimately contribute to building one powerful and collective vision. And it does so in a way that ensures everyone shares their ideas and listens to everyone else's. At the same time, the process provides the speed and agility organizations need to create relevant, agile, and viable plans.

We have seen the benefits of applying LEGO® SERIOUS PLAY® in project management. Most Brazilians love being involved and are eager to join a team, making project team building a relatively easy task on paper. The downside becomes clear when you couple the cultural resistance to long-term planning with the reluctance to use the word *no*. Team members do not fully commit to completing tasks, being held accountable, or meeting deadlines. They are overloaded with tasks. This makes project planning, execution, monitoring, and controlling projects both unreliable and complicated.

As certified LEGO® SERIOUS PLAY® facilitators, we are trained to design workshops that provide a safe environment. It is our job to ensure people feel free to vent about problematic issues. We must encourage participants to focus on both long- and short-term solutions. These conversations are vital to getting the type of vision and buy-in we need from the participants to define tasks and take on the responsibilities to deliver on them.

Additionally, when using LSP in the initiation and planning phases of project management, people frequently build important relationships. This can give team members and project managers the confidence to speak up when necessary. This may come into play when parts of the project deviate from the vision, when there is a significant change in resource availability, or when new opportunities for improvement arise. All of this translates into the speed and adaptability required to be successful in a VUCA atmosphere.

In Brazil, there is currently a strong entrepreneurship movement. This has created a growing demand for the development of small and micro-entrepreneurs. In our experience, we have found they can benefit from LEGO® SERIOUS PLAY® in several ways. Many individuals are looking to design their businesses, assess scenarios, and design solutions in response to economic changes. Specifically, we have found LSP allows them to reflect on their skills, better evaluate situations, assess stakeholder needs, and improve processes and relationships with customers and suppliers.

CONCLUSION

We are grateful for the participants and facilitators we have been given the opportunity to get to know and work with using LEGO® SERIOUS PLAY® in Brazil. They have repeatedly shown us not only the beauty, greatness and creativity of the Brazilian people but also the power that lies in LEGO® SERIOUS PLAY® methods when it comes to playing with the purpose of reflecting, sharing stories, building relationships, cultivating creativity and, of course, solving problems.

The Brazilian singer and song writers Gonzaguinha said it well in his song "O que É, O Que É", in which he encourages others to live life without being ashamed of being happy and to sing to the beauty being eternal learners. We consider ourselves perpetual students and have much more to learn about LEGO® SERIOUS PLAY®, cultural diversity, leadership, team and organizational development and life in general. We can't wait to see what we all build together next!

4

CANADA: THE TRUE NORTH, CREATIVE AND FREE

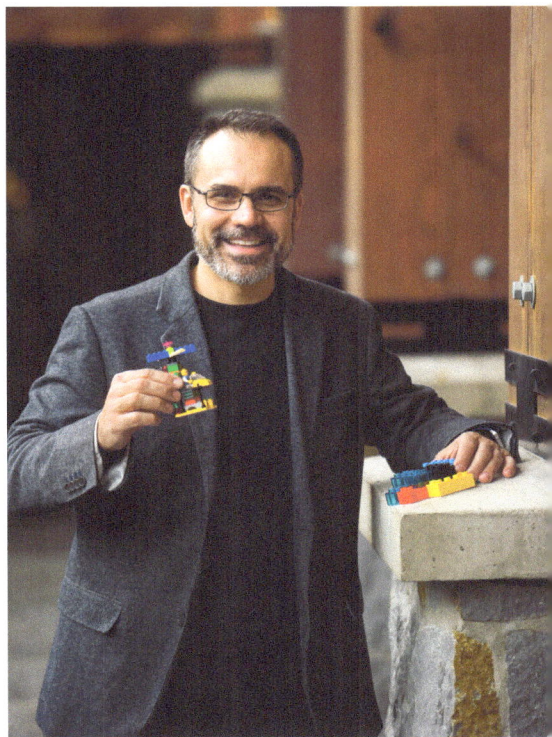

By Jacqueline Lloyd Smith & Collaborator Sébastien Giroux

I first read about LSP in my MBA Program at Royal Roads University, which I worked on from 2004 – 2006. I was studying to become an Executive Management Consultant. My graduation goal was to utilize both my MBA and my 15-plus years of experience as an art and play therapist, along with my previous training and MA in Conflict Analysis and Management.

In 2005, I read a small finance article about mergers and acquisitions. The writer acknowledged that very little was being done to support the people and the culture during these financially driven processes; too much energy was focused on bricks and mortar. They had my attention. One sentence mentioned the LEGO® company was working on an application that could help during the process, by dealing with the people issues created by mergers and acquisitions. I immediately had ideas on how I could put my MBA to good use.

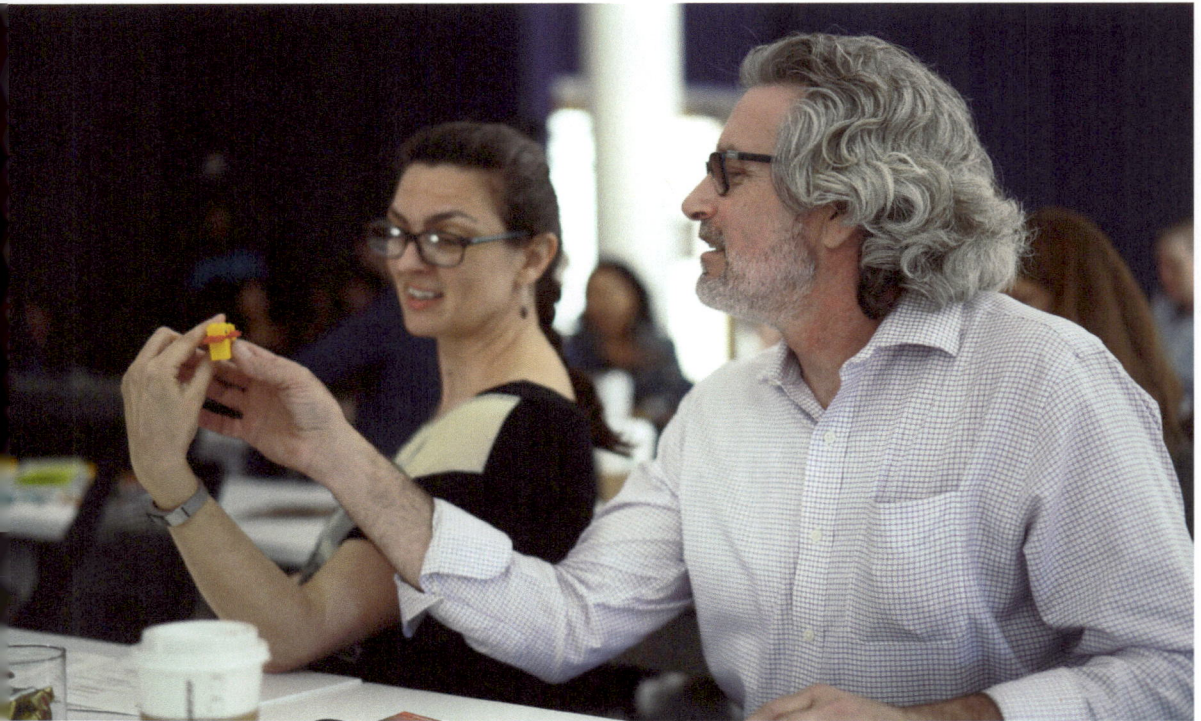

My name is Jacqueline Lloyd Smith. I would like to share how LEGO® SERIOUS PLAY® methods (LSP), got its start in Canada. I will also provide insight into how new facilitators can introduce innovative and novel tools into a more conservative or traditional market.

When I discovered LEGO® SERIOUS PLAY® in university, I knew I had stumbled onto something very interesting. I had no idea then how this small article would change the direction of my life's work and my life overall. For six months, I wrote emails and made phone calls until I finally found the right person at the LEGO® company in Denmark: Jesper Just Jensen.

Jesper had just joined LEGO® as the Director of the SERIOUS PLAY® division, and he was happy to share what he knew about the program. The details were not completely clear to me, but it was obvious the training program and the license were going to be expensive. I also could not identify a clear ROI. However, I was certain I could use it in my work. I was consulting in boardrooms that desperately needed help to improve their processes of communication, thinking, and decision-making. This application sounded as close to anything I had found that included the highly effective techniques of art and play therapy.

At this time, the only way to be trained in LSP was to apply and be vetted by LEGO®. It was Jesper Just Jensen who deemed me to be an appropriate candidate, and he invited me to join the program. Little did I know this telephone meeting with Jesper would lead to a lifelong friendship. Jesper was and continues to be a thoughtful and reflective practitioner, not to mention a wonderful leader. LEGO® offered the training in two locations: Enfield, Connecticut, at their North American headquarters; and in Billund, Denmark, at their corporate headquarters. I took the training in Enfield, and the next year I traveled to Denmark to attend the partner meetings and learning days, which has since morphed into the LEGO® Idea Conference. This is where I first meet Jesper.

In 2006, I became the first business owner to successfully bring LEGO® SERIOUS PLAY® methods to Canada under the LEGO® SERIOUS PLAY® licensed model. My extensive experience in art and play therapy, along with my MBA, made for an easy transition. I was immediately getting great results. I did not try to sell LEGO® to anyone. I simply added it to my tool kit and then used it unapologetically with all my business clients. My best line was, "Don't think of this as a toy. Think of this tool as a plastic-molded 3D-modeling system for communication and learning transfer." At first, I used LSP as an ice-breaker activity, but people did not want to put the bricks away. So I kept adding more and more, until finally people started to call me because I had this cool and engaging way to work with groups: the LSP application.

Around this time, Jesper asked me to represent LEGO® at a number of large and important conferences. He wanted me to showcase the tool and get it into the hands of more people. I was happy to do this, and I travelled in and out of the USA to attend interesting conferences they were sponsoring. I embraced all the opportunities to meet with other creative minds, working hard at getting as many people as possible to use the bricks and experience the power of play. Soon I was being asked to give keynotes, run breakouts, and speak on the power of serious play methods while meeting some of the world's leaders in creative thinking and innovation. LEGO® SERIOUS PLAY® was innovative and leading edge, and creative thought leaders were beginning to take notice. It was still, however, way ahead of its time.

In April of 2007, the LEGO® SERIOUS PLAY® Division of the LEGO® Systems Group awarded my business start-up with a partner award for new business growth and development. In the fall of 2007, Jesper Just Jensen trusted me to train others in this method of LSP outside of the usual two training locations, which was a bit of an experiment. In 2008, our company was named the lead LSP business for Canada. In 2009, I was appointed to the LSP training board with three other associates. Together, we not only improved the training process and consulted on the content of the LSP kits, but we also worked on the idea of moving LSP into the world with no license agreements, which is now the open-source model. As the Play4Business training board members for the LEGO® SERIOUS PLAY® division, we were all trained to train others in LSP. We were named LEGO® SERIOUS PLAY® Master Trainers, a title the four of us still use to this day.

In 2010, after Jesper moved to the Education division, LEGO® Play4Business took over the LEGO® Serious Play® division and made the process 100% open source. They decided to stop training in LSP and to let the newly minted Master Trainers instruct others under their own company names. In early 2011, I ran the first LSP certification training in Canada under the newly developed open-source model I helped to design.

It did not take long for people to take notice that a Canadian company was training people in LEGO® SERIOUS PLAY® methods. Because Canada has such an excellent reputation, both in diplomacy and education, leaders and innovators from around the world were attracted to our training. Canada continually ranks in the top 5 in the world for education, on the scales of access and quality.[9] Our second training brought people from Brazil, Chile, the U.S., and Canada. We then traveled to Panama, where we ran our first international training. Procter & Gamble Venezuela followed, asking us to train their team of expert scientists to use LSP for research and development. This visit led us back to P&G's innovation lab in the

---

[9] Morgan, C. Education in Canada: In Pursuit of Educational Quality & Equity. Spanish Journal of Comparative Education, 2010.

U.S., where we were named best in class by their innovation leadership team. We now partner with an innovation leader at P&G, testing and prototyping new applications to offer and improve our training program.

▬ CANADIANS HAVE AN ABUNDANCE AND INNOVATION IS NOT A NECESSITY ▬

Here are some facts about Canada. It is the second largest country in the world after Russia and borders only one country: the United States of America. We have the longest coastline with 202,080 km or 125, 567 miles of coast. We have half the world's lakes and two of the world's largest lakes. We have a population of around 38 million people but 82% of those people live in the cities, leaving the majority of Canada wide open and full of very small towns and villages. 1.4 million Canadians identify as belonging to indigenous or aboriginal people. The people of Canada have access to an excellent world-class education system, resulting in a very high literacy rate.[10]

---

[10] www.facebook.com/mustdocanada, "201+ Weird, Fun and Interesting Facts About Canada," Must Do Canada, April 5, 2021, https://www.mustdocanada.com/interesting-facts-about-canada.

It is important to remember Canada has two official languages: English and French. French is the first language for about 22.8% of the country's population. 85.4% of French-speaking Canadians live in Quebec, and nearly 10.4 million Canadians are able to converse in French.[11] There has been a significant increase in the number of Canadians who speak both languages. Between 2006 – 2011, the number of bilingual individuals rose by 5.8 million. The majority of these people were from Quebec.[12] These statistics are why, as a Canadian company, we felt it vital to partner with top-notch trainers who can provide the best LSP experience in French.

[11] Canadian Heritage, "Government of Canada," Canada.ca (/ Gouvernement du Canada, September 13, 2019), https://www.canada.ca/en/canadian-heritage/services/official-languages-bilingualism/publications/facts-canadian-francophonie.html.

[12] "Linguistic Characteristics of Canadians," Statistics Canada: Canada's national statistical agency / Statistique Canada : Organisme statistique national du Canada, July 23, 2018, https://www12.statcan.gc.ca/census-recensement/2011/as-sa/98-314-x/98-314-x2011001-eng.cfm.

Canada was founded in 1867, making it a very young country. Our closest neighbor, the U.S., was founded on individual rights and freedoms. In contrast, Canada was founded on the principles of governance, law, and order. Yes, we are a very conservative bunch. Our rich natural resources, such as lumber and minerals, are very attractive commodities in the world market. Large corporations seized on these opportunities, creating many well-paying company jobs offering steady pay and security. The railroad was built to connect the country from coast to coast, in order to transport goods to large shipping ports. From there, they could be exported to the waiting world. Because of the country's vast size and wealth of resources, in the 1800s there was an influx of workers from around the world who were eager to take advantage of the resulting employment opportunities. Canada continues to keep its doors open and has one of the fastest growing populations in the G7.

These circumstances have created a country that develops innovation, but not out of necessity. This is the land of plenty. The country was founded by large corporations working to harvest natural resources, such as the Hudson's Bay Company and the Canadian Pacific Railroad. Canada provides its citizens a great deal of stability. In countries where people do not have this security, people feel a burning need for entrepreneurship, risk-taking, creative thinking, and innovation. Larger centers with a high population allow for greater market knowledge where people share information, creating a spillover effect.[13]

In this light, Canada, and more specifically Thunder Bay, Ontario may not sound like the ideal location to launch something as innovative as LEGO® SERIOUS PLAY®. Yet somehow it worked.

I started my business and introduced LEGO® SERIOUS PLAY® to Canada while I was living in Thunder Bay, Ontario. At the time, the population was about 109,000. To look at a map, the city is a small isolated community in what many call 'the middle of nowhere'; it also has a very cold climate in the winter. The drive to the cities next sizable town is nearly eight hours. The majority of residents work for one of the large private or government corporations. Thunder Bay does not appear to be a strong candidate for such a significant product launch, and yet everything about the location worked. Research conducted by Orlando & Verba found that small and less populated areas work well for start-ups given the lower costs of operating a business, such as rent.[14]

---

[13] Michael J. Orlando & Michael Verba: "Do Only Big Cities Innovate? Technological Maturity and the Location of Innovation". Economic Review 2005

[14] Orlando & Verba, 2005

Jaime Dantas, Wildlife Photographer, https://unsplash.com/@jaimedantas

Canada can be described as a peaceful and stable country, elements necessary for innovation and trade. Canadians think of themselves as rule-based and well-behaved. They are proud to be members of numerous global multilateral organizations, including: G7, G20, NATO, NORAD, UN, WTO, APEC, CETA, and CPTPP. Even though we have some great inventions to our name like basketball, peanut butter, garbage bags, and insulin, we are definitely not as entrepreneurial as our neighbors in the U.S. We continue to struggle to market ourselves and our goods.[15]

People often say Thunder Bay has the feel of a small town, where people know each other and see each other all the time. And in small towns, people exchange information quickly. This is particularly true when they learn about something new and different they think is worth sharing. That is the ideal atmosphere when you want to spread the word about something you like.

The people of Thunder Bay are great at networking, both with each other and with people from outside the region. This geographic location creates both an incubation bubble and also an outreach program that is both organic and powerful. Bringing LSP in with the backing from LEGO® is what made a huge difference in the launch of

---

[15] Robertson, C. Personal Reflections: What Foreign Diplomats Need to Know about Canada. Canadian Global Affairs Institute, 2019.

this tool. People were both curious and supportive. Because the Director of LEGO® SERIOUS PLAY® was also asking me to speak at conferences in the US, I was meeting potential clients from around the world. Soon I was able to start namedropping leaders from large brands who had been testing the tool and loved it. People began to take notice.

Some of the early adopters of this method were the Thunder Bay and region economic development folks who embraced the opportunity to get away from the traditional, boring, and ineffective processes for strategy work. They were the first to test LSP and the first to heavily promote its use in their networks. The Thunder Bay Regional Health Sciences Center was also a great support, and their strong leadership team created an opportunity for their people to engage in an LSP workshop. The informal network of the human resources community quickly shared information, and they supported each other as they introduced the method to their internal teams. Their support was essential to the launch of this method in Canada.

As leaders in their fields, many of the early users of LSP also provided testimonials and case studies to help share their personal experiences and insights. One such testimonial was posted on the LEGO.com/seriousplay website for many years:

> *With captivating simplicity, the workshop was a powerful approach to unlock the full creativity of staff. The progression of skill building exercises creates a uniquely grounding experience of three-dimensional self-discovery interwoven with genuine team values. It was wonderful to see how working with LEGO® SERIOUS PLAY® process allowed staff to tap their creative potential and further the goals of the succession by achieving full contribution by each participant.*

DANIEL MCGOEY, EXECUTIVE DIRECTOR, WESTWAY,
THUNDER BAY, ON, CANADA

LSP was also quickly picked up by the Indigenous organizations in Thunder Bay, which then spread wider throughout Ontario. Because it is such an amazing tool for thinking, communicating, and capturing stories, the use of LSP within this large Canadian demographic works very well. Builders get the opportunity to create something physical and metaphorical to use as a springboard for storytelling. Storytellers are sometimes surprised as they uncover richer details and deeper meaning bubbles to the surface. Research conducted by Anna McNamara, at the University of Surrey in the UK, describes this process well as students use LSP to

unpack the learning process.[16] Within the aboriginal community, we have trained and certified:

- Professionals who coach and support youth emerging from the foster care system.
- Professionals who work in additions counseling.
- First responders who board two engine planes and fly into the most remote small communities in the northwestern regions of Canada.

To launch the application in Canada, and specifically in Thunder Bay, Jesper from the LEGO® Systems Group wrote a wonderful press release announcing our launch. We ran an invitation-only open house, which brought many community leaders in to try LSP for themselves. As people left to head home, we videotaped their testimonials. This created the early buzz we needed. Then via word of mouth, the requests for LSP began to come in. Hats off to everyone who answered that first invitation to join us in Thunder Bay and to the community that helped to get the news out.

[16] Mcnamara, A.: The Use Of LEGO® SERIOUS PLAY® To Enable Learning Gain In Professional Actor Training, University of Surrey, United Kingdom. International Journal of Management and Applied Research, 2018, Vol. 5, No. 4

CANADIANS ARE DIPLOMATIC TO A FAULT!

Canadians have a worldwide reputation for being very nice people. People think of us as diplomatic, polite, patient, tolerant, apologetic, and averse to conflict. We are also known for saying, "I'm sorry," a little too much. Our U.S. neighbors love to tease us for all these things that make us so very Canadian, along with our very conservative values. One time, a friend of mine from the U.S. said, "I'm sorry, okay? Really, I'm Canadian sorry." I still think that is funny.

On the surface, this sounds positive. But there is a downside to it. Canadians do not usually say what they think, at least not in the moment. For example, people tend to keep their complaints to themselves during meetings. They save it for afterward, out in the hallway. They feel a need to solicit others' opinions and thoughts before openly expressing their own grievances. Very nice Canadians can be passive aggressive.

This behavior is cultural, and it is difficult to see or identify certain behaviors when living within a community. To identify those aspects of your own culture, you must leave and observe another to notice the differences. Cultural behaviors stem from values and beliefs. These things make up our identity.

Many people around the world think of Canadians as being very similar to the people of the U.S. But if you ask an American what they think of Canadians, there is a good chance their description will include the word "nice." Canada likes this description. Our leaders are often stating the Canadian values of which they are proud, particularly ones like tolerance.

Of course, we must be careful about stereotyping. It is simply inaccurate to state that all Canadians are one thing or another. Yet most Canadians will agree it is difficult to disagree without appearing disagreeable. They may not want to take on the battle, and they will often sit back and wait before taking action that may come across as aggressive and pushy. As a nation, we are conflict-averse. Many create artificial harmony within their teams or organizations.

Fellow French-Canadian LEGO® SERIOUS PLAY® methods facilitator and trainer, Sebastien Giroux, confirms French speaking Canadians share this desire to avoid conflict. Together, we have co-facilitated in French and English sessions that have been simultaneously translated. In these sessions, we have both observed the same degree of avoidance.

Consider a meeting where there is a hot topic, an elephant in the room so to speak. Asking people to speak directly about the problem is very difficult, because they are concerned they will come across as offensive. They will skirt around the issue and avoid speaking about it directly. And when a conflict does arise, people become very uncomfortable. Chances are, the meeting will be very quiet and end quickly.

Many Canadians opt for avoidance when it comes to conflict. At times, this strategy can be very effective. If the conflict is not that important, then avoidance is a great tactic. If the relationship is not important, avoidance might be the best way forward. If it appears the other side has more power, and a conflict may result in our having even less, avoidance could be an excellent strategy.

Avoidance becomes problematic when we leave issues unaddressed. Over time, people find it more difficult to discuss the problems. Small issues can quickly grow, and then we live in artificial harmony while accomplishing very little.

When we market LEGO® SERIOUS PLAY® method workshops, we state the three big benefits of LSP:

- Insights
- Confidence
- Commitment

For cultures that like to debate and argue, LSP can stop the usual conversational roundabouts or hours of debating for the sake of it. And in risk-averse cultures, LSP can stop the avoidance behavior where people sweep conflicts under the rug. People tend to find it harder to talk about their very strong views and contradicting priorities; instead, they get caught up in debating policy, rules, legislation, etc. [17]

For Canadians, just having the space to talk about their thoughts and ideas through the use of metaphors can be enormously helpful. Within the first few minutes of a workshop, the participants quickly learn a few ground rules that create

---

[17] Rothman, J. Resolving Identity Based Conflict in Nations, Organizations, and Communities. Jossey-Bass 1997.

a safe place to talk and exchange ideas. Some of the items on this list could be considered ground rules, while others fall more into the category of etiquette:

1   The model belongs to the builder.
2   Only the model's builder knows the real story and can explain its meaning.
3   Everyone's story is perfect, and everyone has a different story.
4   We do not have to change someone's mind just because they see things differently. It just means they have different ideas
5   To get the most from the group, we need to hear every story.
6   The value of the group comes from the diversity of thought.
7   Everyone builds and everyone tells their story.
8   We encourage participants to speak from the heart.

We also have several rules to keep the meeting on track and reinforce that we are here to work:

1   No walking in and out. We take breaks together.
2   No electronics allowed. You need to remain present.
3   Suspend all judgement.
4   Question only the LEGO® bricks.
5   Trust the process.
6   Listen generously to others.

These ground rules and underpinning principals reinforce the Canadian values of inclusion and tolerance, and no one is going to disagree with them. By using LEGO® SERIOUS PLAY®, where people build models as metaphors for discussion and reflection, everyone gets to talk about issues in a way that separates the deed from the doer. This takes conversation to the next level, where ideas from the inside world come to the outside world for exploration and discovery.

Because of my educational background and experience, I have been invited to use LSP as a conflict management tool to unpack some very stubborn conflicts in organizations and communities. It is incredibly powerful when people get to use the bricks to build their differing perspectives of a conflict and then listen to each other's stories. I have taken the bricks into settings where some stakeholders were no longer speaking or even making eye contact.

The process puts the focus of the problems on the 3D models instead of the people. When the builders can begin to point at the tabletop model and see and hear all sides to the conflict situation, they can move the pieces around to compare and contrast their world, community, or team view and experience. As people begin to feel others are hearing them, the room becomes lighter and everyone starts to understand the process is not about winning. It is about accepting that everyone has their own story. The richness of learning is in accepting that all stories are valid, and together the stories weave the current situation (good or bad). Once the situation is built, together the builders can consider how to move forward. This is the first step. Or rather, it is step two. The first step is getting people into the same room.

When conflicts are no longer intractable, this does not mean there is no longer a conflict. Not everything is meant to be resolved in the sense that one party wins and the other loses.[18] To move a conflict forward may mean people are starting to listen. This creates the hope that empathy will follow. All conflicts have high stakes, because the hidden costs of conflict range from people

---

[18] Kriesberg L., Northrup T.A., Thorson S.J., Intractable Conflicts and Their Transformation. Syracuse University Press Syracuse, NY. 1989.

leaving and moving to new employment opportunities to costly union disputes that end up in court. Not to mention all the hidden costs like sick leave and lack of engagement.

■■ CANADIANS TEND TO BE CONSERVATIVE AND RISK AVERSE ■

Unlike many of our clients in the USA, Canadians tend to resist testing or trying something new. They are more likely to try something new if they hear about it from a trusted friend who highly recommends it, or if they read something written by a credible source. They like to test things in a small way before taking any measured risk. And even then, it can be extremely nerve-wracking for the HR leader who makes the decision to try a new process internally. The buzz creates high expectations, and the leader's reputation is on the line.

Getting LSP started in Canada was a long journey, paved by hard work, dedication, and an unshakable faith in the power of the method. Years before COVID-19 and Zoom, sometime around 2006, I flew into Toronto's Lester B. Pearson Airport. On arrival, I rented a car and stayed overnight in a hotel, just to go to a one-hour meeting at the City of Mississauga. I gave the senior team small bags of LEGO® so I could let them experience the power of the method. Five minutes into building, they got it. They knew LSP was the perfect tool to use with the 300 emerging leaders they were bringing to their upcoming leadership meeting.

I knew in my heart if they were able to try the tool, they would be ready to engage our company. I was willing to put in the time and make the investment just to let them experience the power of LSP. In the end, it was a large and successful event. People lined up afterward to thank us for providing the opportunity for them to share their ideas. One woman waited until everyone had left to tell me that she had never spoken at a meeting like this. This was, in fact, the first time she had shared her ideas with others. I think we both had tears in our eyes.

We have so many stories of powerful workshops that end with people thanking us and even hugging us. Over and over, we hear from disconnected staff who tell us they have never before attended anything that ended with any real decision-making. For the first time in their careers, they felt the time they spent working with the group made sense. It resulted in game-changing outcomes that would go on to adjust the way people think, express their ideas, and ultimately change how they work together.

Our French-speaking facilitators have made similar observations. Across the board, Canadians seem willing to attend numerous meetings and engage in long conversations. Yet they are slow to make decisions and take action to move their agendas forward. We begin some of our workshops with teams or groups building a clear and articulated vision. This helps everyone come together to quickly identify their objectives. When using bricks to conduct a gap analysis, we can rapidly pinpoint potential issues; then we use the bricks to find solutions as a group. This whole process allows for stakeholder buy-in from the group, which is necessary for the organization's forward movement.

LEGO® SERIOUS PLAY® methods are an excellent way to add much-needed structure to conversations in meetings and workshops; discussions stay on track and on topic. Our French-Canadian facilitators have had the same experiences in their work. The LEGO® models create placeholders to mark conversations and carry the talks forward. Participants collaborate to discover insights, which changes the conversation and allows them to determine actionable items and make decisions. The entire process gives everyone equal opportunity to have their say and be heard, and it gives them the confidence to move forward by taking measured and reasonable risks.

We also learned the power of volunteering. We did so with many charities like the United Way, in both Canada and the U.S., who needed strategy just like for-profit corporations. Boards are full of hardworking people, who often take our card and then call us to work for their private paying organizations. We have answered almost every request to present LSP at conferences. When we give a keynote, we are more than happy to pack up our bricks and fly to almost any corner of the world. We also run breakouts at conferences, where complete strangers will gather to test out the tool. Sometimes, it takes years before these people circle back. It is not unusual now to get a call from someone who I met years ago at a conference or a meeting, who held onto my card.

One of my favorite stories is from the City of Surrey, where a new learning and development manager, Falina Stack, found my card in her desk and called to see if I could run a learning session on creativity. However, before officially booking us she needed to bring us to the city's head office for a meeting. With the amazing support and clarity of vision from the city manager, she booked us for a 3-day retreat. Since her first phone call, many leaders from the City of Surrey have participated in workshops, retreats, and strategy sessions where we have used LSP to unpack complicated problems and prototype new ideas. We have worked on a range of issues, including poverty reduction, the creation of low-cost homes, daycare, crime reduction, neighborhood engagement, and repurposing libraries. The city leadership teams have provided us with testimonials and even allowed us to make videos of some of our workshops for marketing and educational purposes. This type of partnership is invaluable to us, because we continue to add to the body of knowledge regarding successful applications of LSP.

Here is a testimonial from Falina Stack, Organizational Development Manager, City of Surrey:

> *The City of Surrey consistently works to innovate in an effort to best serve our residents in an evolving landscape. Jacquie and Stephen led our team through the Serious Play problem solving model, which stretched our thinking and perceptions of innovation in ways that we didn't expect. The outcome was a highly engaged team that felt that they had all contributed to solving sticky problems with tangible outputs that were immediately usable by the city. Not only did the sessions stretch us as a team, they reshaped the way that we approach challenges as a city.*

But the question still remains: How can a creative facilitator enter a conservative market when that market might not be ready for an innovative and creative tool that has such a strong brand association with a toy? This can definitely be a puzzle. People often call us when they realize what they are doing is no longer working for them. Or when then just don't know what to do next and they feel like they have already tried everything.

One way to get people to play along is to downplay the tool and focus on the results. Stressing the results gets people interested, especially when we provide financial figures or the return on investment of working with us. We often name-drop or provide testimonials from our larger US clients as evidence this method drives results when led by an experienced facilitator. Here is one testimonial from Richard Perez, the general manager of Procter & Gamble's Innovation Gym. We proudly use this testimonial to help us enter more conservative settings:

> In my experience Strategic Play has been very effective to create physical constructs/artifacts among senior executives to represent complex problems and strategies that enable deep conversations leading to new insights and strategies. I really value the methodology of LEGO® SERIOUS PLAY® for enabling conversations free of bias and the flexibility to create scenario simulations in real time in a very simple and practical way. These scenarios are instrumental in creating robust strategies in multidimensional situations that are difficult to examine with traditional board meetings. The fun and engaging elements of the methodology are nice "icing on the cake", the real benefit is the breakthrough insights that are discovered leading to more robust business strategies. Having Jacquie and her team facilitate brings the experience to the next level. Jacquie brings a wealth of business application experience together with a masterful ability to sense the audience and course correct on the spot to achieve the desired outcomes. As part of my role I benchmark and validate Best in Class strategic partners on Innovation. I can say that Jacquie's organization is Best in Class.

When you are working in a country like Canada, where the business world is rather conservative, the key to selling LSP is *not selling it*. LSP is a tool, not the product you are selling. Facilitators using this tool need to sell the outcome. I do a full sales presentation for new facilitators where I break this down. At first, new facilitators are so enamored by the LEGO® name and logo they only want to put photos of LEGO® bricks on their website and marketing materials. They try to lead with LEGO® SERIOUS PLAY® , which no one can understand from photos. Not only do photos of the LEGO® bricks not sell to adults working in business settings, due to the strong association with the toy element, but there are trademark infractions that do not go unnoticed by the LEGO® Systems Group, who kindly allow us to use this method. Our team does its best to educate and inform others and tell them about our failures in thinking when we first started.

It does not matter where you are located. Remember this: You will sabotage yourself by trying to sell LEGO® SERIOUS PLAY® workshops by using photos of bricks, Minifigures, or the trade name. That simply will not work. From our years of experience in Canada, we feel confident in asserting the only way you can sell this method is to explain and demonstrate the method's powerful outcomes, preferably while getting the bricks into your prospects' hands.

I believe LSP is a tool that should be in every facilitator's tool kit, just like a marker or Post-it Notes. I tell potential clients about the results we get, not about the tool we use. In some fear-based firms and organizations, this may not be enough. They might also need to touch the bricks and build with them to really understand the power of the process though their own storytelling. Because most people have become so accustomed to teleconferencing, it is even easier: Mail a bag of LEGO® to your potential users and do a live online demonstration. You need to be creative while getting their hands on the bricks.

CONCLUSION

Living in Canada has been a gift. By working in a location where people are conservative and reluctant to try new things, we have been forced to become creative in our attempts to inform via sharing the method. We quickly learned word-of-mouth marketing is by far the most powerful way to spread the message. We have been able to show the market how we use this tool through case studies and testimonials, supplemented with professional photos of people building and storytelling. However, getting the bricks into people's hand is the fastest way to their hearts and minds. And nothing can replace the powerful assistance of informal leaders who are willing and ready to share the good news.

Working with such an innovative tool, you must be able to show potential clients examples and solid results. We do this by sharing strong testimonials and stories from the field. If you are working in a more traditional marketplace, look around your landscape and talk to leaders. Listen between the lines for clues as to what really keeps them awake at night. In Canada, these stories seem to revolve around:

1   Intractable team and organizational conflicts.
2   Getting stuck on the same problems

3 Speeding up innovation and then getting the innovation to market.

4 Developing and telling compelling stories to engage internal stakeholders and external potential customers

5 Continuing to create ideas for solid marketing plans that will drive Canadian companies and organizations into a shoulder-to-shoulder market position with their neighbors.

LEGO® SERIOUS PLAY® can be a hugely valuable tool to address many of these sticky business issues. Even the most conservative and risk averse organizations and leaders are looking to try something that will work and deliver results. Nobody wants a boring meeting, workshop, or off-site where circular conversations prevent people from developing and implementing brilliant strategy.

5

CHINA:
THE COMPLEXITY OF PERCEPTION

By Brian Tang

"Perception is reality," as the saying goes. Our perception shapes our thoughts, decision-making, and behaviors. The Coca-Cola brand could mean happiness for you, and it could imply guilty pleasure for me. It could mean 100 different things to 100 different people. Who is right? We are all right, because the difference of interpretation is rooted in different perceptions. There is no right answer for it. Some perceptions may be biased; but again, it does not matter. Perception is reality. We tend to believe our own perceptions are true, and that others' perceptions are not.

I will discuss how perception is heavily shaped by cultural and local factors in the areas of China, Hong Kong, and Macau. My name is Brian Tang and I am from Macau. I am a licensed trainer and certified facilitator of the LEGO® SERIOUS PLAY® method. Before I devoted my career to the LSP method, I was working in-house for a leading integrated resort in Macau. I have over a decade of experience in the corporate learning and development field, including operations training, leadership development, blended learning, program design and development, and trainers' development programs. I have also taught a BBA program in a tertiary institute.

Since becoming a licensed trainer of the LEGO® SERIOUS PLAY® methodology, I have devoted my time to training people to become certified facilitators of the method. I have conducted LSP workshops across Macau, Hong Kong, and China. I was raised in Macau, a very tiny piece of land adjacent to Hong Kong. Both Hong Kong and Macau are now Special Administrative Regions of China. They were

both returned to the motherland by the U.K. and Portugal in 1997 and 1999, respectively. The geographical proximity and similarities in social and cultural factors across the three locations makes it easy for me to develop and penetrate the markets. However, even areas with similar cultural backgrounds can produce very different perceptions, as we will explore further. Specifically, you will discover how people from this part of the world come across the LEGO® brand and the LSP method, how they see the value of certification from the Western world, and how people's learning expectations in the classroom may pose challenges to the facilitator. I will cover best practices to help address these challenges.

You will never come across someone who tells you to your face, "My perception on ABC is XYZ." To discover and synthesize people's perceptions, you need to read between the lines and be very observant of their behaviors. Self-reflection and keeping a curious mind are critical in identifying perceptions. I will summarize my experience in the learning and training field in Macau, Hong Kong, and China through the lens of using the LSP method. I will give a behind-the-scenes look at the many lessons I have learned, which involved a great deal of blood, sweat, and tears. I hope to bring you interesting and refreshing perspectives on why people believe or behave in certain ways. You may even learn to better leverage people's perceptions to your own advantage.

▬▬ PERCEPTIONS OF THE LEGO® BRAND ▬▬

LEGO® is a well-known brand across the world. However, its name recognition has varied in different regions and time periods. Thanks to Hong Kong's international exposure and relatively strong economic power from the 1980s onward, the LEGO® brand has quickly gained traction. Countless kids love playing with the high quality and creative toys, and parents are willing to shell out their hard-earned money. Keep in mind, however, not all families are able to afford the toy. Over a few decades, the LEGO® brand has become a household name in Hong Kong. As a result, there is a strong base of LEGO® fans in Hong Kong and Macau.

Although I grew up playing with LEGO®, it was not until I began to promote the LEGO® SERIOUS PLAY® method in Hong Kong and Macau that I realized the extent of the public's perceptions of the brand. When I asked participants why they came to my workshop, many of them answered that they love playing with LEGO® bricks. They had never heard of the LSP method prior to my workshop and they certainly did not come to experience LSP. They came because the workshop was about LEGO®. This certainly worked to my advantage. Psychologist Robert Zajonc has coined the term "Mere Exposure Effect"[19], which states people tend to like things with which they are familiar. When I introduced the LSP method to the markets, I quickly drew people's attention to it because of its association with LEGO®. Because most people are already familiar with the brand, it was not so hard for them to learn a new methodology that is associated with it.

The LEGO® SERIOUS PLAY® method benefits from people's perceptions of the LEGO® brand—fun, creative, and quality. They tend to associate these attributes with the LSP method and my workshops. More subtly, the registered symbol "®" behind the words LEGO® and SERIOUS PLAY® gives people a perception of authenticity and quality. These perceptions gave me a comparative advantage to introduce this creative problem-solving tool to the market, as opposed to a lesser-known methodology. In short, it was a relatively easy sell for me.

The picture in mainland China was quite different from that of Hong Kong. Today, China is the second largest economy in the world.[20] The China market is the strategic growth engine for the LEGO® Group.[21] However, this was hardly the case a few decades back. Today's affluent parents may fill their kids' toy corners with LEGO®, but most never got to play with the bricks when they were small. They simply could not afford it, or it may not have even been available in the market. I learned the market in mainland China did not have the same strong adult fan base I was accustomed to. The Mere Exposure Effect was much less apparent in China when compared to Hong Kong and Macau.

Although perceptions of the LEGO® brand and its positive attributes have been advantageous to my bringing LSP to the market here, sometimes it has been a double-edged sword. LEGO® bricks are firmly entrenched in people's minds as just a toy. People have a hard time seeing there is educational value in playing with the same toy their kids are playing with every day. They do not understand how senior executives can be playing with these bricks in the boardroom. In the Chinese culture, play is traditionally seen as the opposite of hard work. There is an old Chinese proverb: Working hard gives you results; play is of no value. Another similar proverb is: People addicted to play will lose their aspirations. As you can see, the Chinese culture hardly encourages play; children learn this in their upbringing. Therefore, consciously and subconsciously, the Chinese tend to disregard the idea of value in play. While there is a certain degree of truth to

---

[19] "APA PsycNet," American Psychological Association (American Psychological Association), accessed July 7, 2021, https://psycnet.apa.org/record/1968-12019-001.

[20] https://www.nasdaq.com/articles/the-5-largest-economies-in-the-world-and-their-growth-in-2020-2020-01-22

[21] https://asiatimes.com/2019/09/lego-reports-strong-consumer-sales-in-china/

this, modern pedagogy and the recent trend of gamification have revealed the power of play in adult learning.[22] This is now an irreversible trend.

How did I help people get over their misgivings about using bricks in workshops and trainings? I usually play a couple of simple *What the Duck* activities with clients, which helps them to easily see the value of play. [23] As soon as I became a certified facilitator of the LSP method, I made a habit of always carrying a few bags of ducks in my backpack. You just never know when you are going to bump into an ex-colleague, a friend, or a potential client who asks, "Brian, what do you do with the LEGO® thing?" to which I reply, "Do you have a few minutes? Let's play."

People will not simply believe something because you tell them. They will believe when they experience the "Aha" moment for themselves. After a few minutes of playing with the duck, I usually point out, "We have played with just six bricks for a couple minutes, and you have already had some moments of insight. Imagine if we played with a lot more bricks for a few hours or more." This is where their perceptions start to change.

ASSOCIATION WITH INTERNATIONAL BRANDS AND CERTIFICATION

When a brand is perceived as a local brand, people want to see it being adopted locally. When the brand is international, people expect it to be adopted worldwide. Since the LEGO® SERIOUS PLAY® method bears the LEGO® brand, people want to see how it is being adopted on a global scale. For this reason, I highlight to my clients and workshop participants that the LSP methodology originated in the Western world and has been widely adopted by Fortune 500 companies such as Google and Microsoft. People generally perceive that because the methodology comes from the big brand LEGO® and it is being used by well-known companies around the world, it must be good. This is the "Authority Effect" of persuasion by Dr. Robert Cialdini.[24] Leveraging on people's perceptions by highlighting how the method has been used worldwide, and dropping some big names, can increase the credibility of your service offering.

---

[22] Marcy Polack et al., "The Right Brain Develops First ~ Why Play Is the Foundation for Academic Learning," Vince Gowmon, June 16, 2021, https://www.vincegowmon.com/the-right-brain-develops-first/.

[23] *Strategic Play: The Creative Facilitator's Guide #2: What the Duck!* by Jacqueline Lloyd Smith, Denise Meyerson, Stephen Walling

[24] https://www.influenceatwork.com/principles-of-persuasion/#authority

While mentioning worldwide usage may be helpful in securing buy-in from prospects, it is only half the picture. People also want to see local success stories. They can be skeptics about how something that works in the Western world will be successful within their own culture. It is human tendency to think we are different and unique compared to others. Therefore, it is important to be able to show testimonials from local brands to show how it can succeed. Again, this is tapping into the Mere Exposure Effect. People tend to like things they are familiar with: If local brands are buying into the service, it might work in my company too. People want to see evidence it works globally and locally, so it is advisable to show testimonials from both global and local brands.

At the beginning of the chapter, I said sometimes perceptions are incorrect. Interestingly, what I do not tell my clients is that you actually do not need to find the right culture for this creative method to work. When you design and facilitate it properly, the LEGO® SERIOUS PLAY® method *will* work in any culture and locality. This is because the methodology is rooted in human biology and psychology rather than in any cultural behaviors.

Constructionism, constructivism, hand-brain connection, flow, and storytelling are universal. The magic formula is based on rigorous research in neuroscience, psychology, and educational theories; they apply to the human species regardless of cultural factors. I am not suggesting cultural factors are unimportant. They are important in workshop design and facilitation and should be carefully considered by the facilitator. But once you have that nailed, you *will* see a fantastic result from your LSP workshop. We have seen countless success stories across continents, languages, and ethnicities.

The second association I want to talk about is the certification of the LSP method. We at the Strategic Play® Group offer certified training in the LSP method around the world. People who complete the requirements of the training will receive a certificate issued by Strategic Play Global, which is based in Canada. For the training participants in China, Hong Kong, and Macau, the certificate from Strategic Play Global is everything. People in this part of the world heavily favor international certification over local counterparts. People who attend expensive trainings here expect to receive a certificate issued by a foreign association. To be blunt, nobody cares about a certificate issued by a local institute or training provider unless it is accredited by a local education or vocational system. As a training provider, if all you can offer is a certificate issued by your local institute, you may have a hard time selling it. By contrast, if you can bring an international certificate into your program, people will perceive it as credible and valuable. They will be willing to have their credit card ready for payment. There is a saying that Hong Kong people

have a "stamp collection" attitude towards self-development. They collect one certificate after another as if it were a hobby, and they show off their collection on résumés and LinkedIn profiles. The size of your collection can positively influence how employers and clients perceive your skills and level of competitiveness.

To take advantage of the demand for international certificates, some programs in Hong Kong offer it as an add-on item. For example, you pay X amount to attend a program. By the end of it, you will receive a certificate issued by the local training provider. For an additional fee, you will also receive a certificate issued by the international association/institute. Guess what? 10 out of 10 participants will pay for the international certificate. The training provider can market the program at the lower, more attractive amount. But they will still earn the larger fee.

Another subtle perception is the Strategic Play® brand, as a Canadian company, adds an additional level of credibility and perceived quality. Since the 1990s, Canada has been a popular destination for immigration from this part of the world. Many affluent families from China, Hong Kong, and Macau have either emigrated or sent their kids to Canada to pursue quality education and lifestyles. In 2017, China ranked as #1 in terms of country of citizenship among international students studying in Canada, accounting for 28% of the total.[25] Another survey reveals that

---

[25] https://cbie.ca/wp-content/uploads/2018/09/International-Students-in-Canada-ENG.pdf

academic reputation is the #1 factor influencing why international students chose Canada as their destination of study, with 82% of respondents saying this was either essential (36%) or very important (46%).[26] Being a Canadian company in the field of education and training, the Strategic Play® brand certainly benefits from this perception. When we market the LSP certification training as Canadian certified, people buy into its high quality and credibility. Our programs were written by an expert curriculum designer and are delivered by highly qualified trainers. You can take advantage of people's perceptions at the beginning, but you must be able to deliver on their expectations to maintain trust.

Case in point, a methodology called Quantum Speed Reading (QSR) quickly gained a lot of traction in the mainland China market in 2019. This methodology claimed children could read up to 100,000 words in a book in 10 minutes, understand the content, and retain the memory. How does it work? Rather than read, the individual rapidly flips through the pages with their thumb, much like shuffling playing cards. [27] Sound unbelievable? Many parents in China believed in it and they were willing to send their kids to the QSR training camp, which costs several thousand dollars. However, there has not been any solid evidence or third-party verification of this methodology's validity.[28]

Why are Chinese parents willing to spend their hard-earned money on this self-proclaimed, seemingly magical program? First of all, "tiger parents" in China very badly want to see their kids succeed. The earlier they can pave a successful path for the kids, the better. Their children get a head start over others by learning new skills, and having better skills is essential. Second, and more importantly, Quantum Speed Reading was founded by a Japanese educator who has written a book on the topic. When a program is marketed as "Founded in Japan," the whole thing becomes credible. Japan is renowned for its obsession with quality and craftmanship. When the method is founded in Japan, who would doubt its credibility? The training camp providers certainly knew how to take advantage of the Made in Japan perception. However, after the story became widely published by the media, education bureaus in different parts of China halted the QSR training camps[29.] You can leverage on perception, but your deliverables must be credible and of good quality.

---

[26] https://cbie.ca/wp-content/uploads/2018/08/Student_Voice_Report-ENG.pdf

[27] "Quantum Speed Reading (QSR) Is a Completely New Technique for Reading Books without Looking at the Pages.," Quantum Speed Reading, accessed July 7, 2021, https://www.quantumspeedreading.com/.

[28] Zhilin He, "'Quantum Speed Reading' Training Camp Scam Tiger Parents for Thousands of Dollars," chinaSMACK, November 1, 2019, https://www.chinasmack.com/quantum-speed-reading-training-camp-scam-tiger-parents-for-thousands-of-dollars.

[29] https://www.bbc.com/zhongwen/trad/chinese-news-50312390

PERCEPTIONS ON THE ROLE OF THE FACILITATOR AND LEARNING EXPECTATIONS

The third and final perception I want to talk about is learning expectations in the classroom. If you have attended LSP workshops or you are a certified facilitator of the method, you will know the beauty of the methodology lies in its ability to align people's thoughts, to creatively and collectively solve problems, and to unlock insights and wisdom that would have otherwise been locked in people's subconscious minds. One of the foundational principles of the LEGO® SERIOUS PLAY® method is "the answer is in the room," meaning the participants are the best people to answer the question at hand. For example, a facilitator is to use the LSP method to run a strategic re-planning workshop for company ABC in the aftermath of the COVID-19 crisis. The facilitator certainly does not have the answer to the question at hand. The challenge should be, and must be, answered by the workshop participants. The facilitator's job is to run the carefully designed activities with professional yet flexible facilitation skills. This allows the participants to engage in a series of activities and co-create their answer as the workshop progresses. The facilitator is to, literally, facilitate, which is defined by Cambridge Dictionary as: To make something possible or easier. The role of the facilitator is "Guide on the side," ensuring the collective learning outcome is achieved. The learning outcome is therefore an output. By following and facilitating a series of carefully designed activities, the learning outcome is a collective output of discussion, debate, insight, and personal reflection from all participants. These are the characteristics and strength of a LEGO® SERIOUS PLAY® workshop.

When I run LSP workshops in Hong Kong, Macau, and China, however, there are differences. For example, I once ran an LSP creative problem-solving workshop in Hong Kong. The topic was: How can we nurture our kids so they can be best prepared to face future challenges? This is a typical open-ended topic with no clear answers. The workshop ran three hours, and at the end we came up with a list of fantastic ideas involving different stakeholders. After drafting the action plan, I wrapped up the workshop. Participants said it was a great experience playing and problem-solving with LEGO® bricks, but they expected real answers. Comments included:

- Is that it?
- I thought we were going to learn a tool, such as the Fishbone Diagram, so we can use it to problem-solve in the future.
- Where's the learning?
- Too much playing, too little learning.

That was some of the general feedback I got from participants attending my LSP workshops here. In short, people expected to see more concrete answers in the workshop, and the answers better come from the facilitator. This expectation clearly contradicts what I mentioned earlier about how the facilitator does not have the answer to the challenge question.

What happened? And what can we do?

Again, it is about perception. This time, it is about the perception of the role of the facilitator, trainer, and teacher. In the Chinese culture, studying and learning are highly regarded activities. An old Chinese proverb says: Learning is the only important thing; everything else is inferior. As a result, teachers and scholars have long been highly respected in Chinese society. Students are taught to greet, respect, and listen to whatever the teacher has to say. Another proverb tells us how much the Chinese culture respects teachers: He who teaches me for a day is my father for life. Although the culture has developed since ancient times, the new generation is still deeply influenced by these attitudes. For example, students are rarely encouraged to debate with their teacher today. Students who disagree or debate with the teacher are labeled as naughty, and may therefore receive disciplinary actions.

The perceptions shape behaviors of both young students and adults. For example, people in China generally call me Teacher Tang, regardless of whether I am delivering a training, workshop, or simply giving a keynote speech. When I ask them to call me Brian instead, they feel uncomfortable. The implication of the long-entrenched perception of teacher is that people expect the person on the stage to be teacher or trainer, to give them the answer. The role of facilitator is no longer "Guide on the side" but "Sage on the stage," someone who knows the answers— at least partially. Participants expect the learning outcome to be an input, i.e., the trainer will give them the answer rather than expecting them to co-create the answer themselves. The concept of facilitated learning in which the facilitator's job is only to facilitate the learning process as participants come up with answers on their own is fairly new in China. It has yet to be widely accepted there.

So how do we address this perception to our advantage? I have learned to do two things:

1   Manage learning expectations. At the beginning of a workshop, I make it clear to participants the workshop is not a sit-down lecture. It is learning by participation. I also tell them I am not a topic master but a process master; I am only here to facilitate a collective success. In addition, I invite the person who hired me (usually the HR Director or Senior Executive of the company) to make an opening remark at the beginning of the workshop, and to ask participants to work hard together in order to achieve the best outcome. It is extremely important to frame the workshop at the beginning to shape people's expectations.

2   I have learned to incorporate some frameworks and theories into the workshop so there is some predetermined takeaway by the end of the workshop. For example, I introduced the "9 Best Practices of Innovation" in my Innovation workshop. When I talked about building trust in a corporate environment, I talked about the Johari Window and how they could use it on their own. In a corporate strategy making workshop, I brought in the Value Proposition Canvas. When participants know they are following a framework or a theory, they feel they will somehow get the answer; this decreases their anxiety and increases engagement. The framework or theory I introduce becomes what the Chinese call "Dry Goods," some takeaway they can put to use right away. As one participant put it, "I might not have LEGO® bricks to play with when I go back to work, but at least I have learned some best practices of innovation."

In summary, to win over the teacher perception in the Chinese market, LSP facilitators must be equipped with a combination of the LSP methodology and a wide range of other skills and knowledge. Successful workshops require a mix of facilitated learning and teaching.

■ CONCLUSION ■

"Everything we hear is an opinion, not a fact.
Everything we see is a perspective, not the truth."

—ATTRIBUTED TO MARCUS AURELIUS

We have looked at a number of common perceptions of the people in Hong Kong, Macau, and China. We have seen how international and well-known brands such as LEGO® give people an impression of credibility. The perception of Global v. Local tells us the importance of featuring both international and local adoption of the methodology. The perception of LEGO® as a toy instead of an educational tool

can be overcome by the mighty What the Duck. We have learned the importance of the highly favored international certification. And when we are able to benefit from such perceptions, it is vital to deliver from the perspectives of both business ethics and sustainability. Finally, we have explored how the deeply rooted teacher's role shapes people's learning expectations in the classroom and how we, as the facilitator of the LEGO® SERIOUS PLAY® method, can best tackle it.

Perception is a complicated thing. It is shaped by a mix of factors including culture, history, language, and habit. As you might imagine, it is hard—extremely hard—to change perception. Think of perception as the wave in the ocean and you are the surfer. You cannot change the direction of the wave and it is very difficult to surf against it. It is dangerous to do that, by the way. However, if you surf along the wave, you will enjoy a smooth ride. The same goes with perception. It is best to manage and leverage on it, not to change it.

Now that you are aware of some perceptions in this part of the world, let us go out and take the world of play by storm.

6

GERMANY: USING CREATIVITY TO BREAK DOWN STEREOTYPES

By Sven Poguntke

When applying the LEGO® SERIOUS PLAY® method in Germany, I give special consideration to cultural characteristics. Through examples, I will show the importance of etiquette, behavior, and values that are particularly important in a business context in this country. I will examine the possible benefits this method can provide when considered against behaviors regarded as typically German. To do this, I will present a case study of conflict management in the context of East versus West Germany. This will vividly illustrate the cultural clichés and peculiarities that can cause differences of opinion, which can quickly escalate if not addressed. LSP provides the opportunity for a more in-depth analysis of challenges and identifies problem areas that are not immediately obvious at first glance

I would like to take the opportunity to introduce myself and share my story with LSP. I studied business administration at the University of Mannheim (one of the most renowned universities in Germany for this academic field) and at the University of North Carolina, in the USA. At UNC, in the 1990s, research focused on creativity and the involvement of users in the innovation process; this was a precursor of today's design thinking.

My professional career has led me to a renowned management consultancy, where I frequently facilitate workshops in the context of creative problem solving. Since 2004, I have been working as a freelance consultant, management trainer, facilitator, keynote speaker, and book author. My book, *Corporate Think Tanks,* has already been published in its 3rd edition on the German speaking market. In addition, I am an honorary professor for Design Thinking and Innovation at the Media Campus of the University of Applied Sciences in Darmstadt. I am a certified Design Sprint Master and SCRUM Master, as well as a graduate of Alex Osterwalder's Masterclass for Business Model Canvas and Value Proposition Design.

In all my fields of activity, creative methods and approaches play a decisive role. I first heard about LSP in 2011 and was immediately inspired by the idea of using Lego, metaphors, and storytelling for business challenges. One year later, I was certified as an LSP facilitator in Denmark. I have since been able to apply LSP in numerous workshops and university classes as well as at large events. In 2018, I began my collaboration with Strategic Play Global, which operates as SPG Europe in the EU. I am proud to be a part of this innovative trainer community and to be able to exchange ideas with colleagues from all over the world, as well as to contribute to training the next generation of certified facilitators for LSP.

■■■ BUSINESS CULTURE IN GERMANY: ETIQUETTE, BEHAVIORS, AND VALUES ■■■

It is always interesting to note the stereotypes attributed to the inhabitants of a particular country or region. On the one hand, they provide foreigners and guests with a certain orientation. And on the other hand, one is very close to prejudices and generalizations. In a business context, certain labels, behaviors, or values are observable, and using methods such as LSP can have a positive impact.

Speaking of clichés, the weekly magazine Spiegel, which is renowned in Germany, asked foreign correspondents who are experts on the country: How are the Germans? What is striking about them?[30] The following are just some of the identified behaviors:

- Frugality: While other nations often live from hand to mouth, politicians and residents of the country often force a low debt level or a high savings rate.

---

[30] Der Spiegel, "Vorurteile Über Deutsche: Gestresst, Humorlos Und Öfter Nackt Als Nötig," DER SPIEGEL (DER SPIEGEL, August 4, 2017), https://www.spiegel.de/spiegel/vorurteile-ueber-deutsche-gestresst-humorlos-und-oefter-nackt-als-noetig-a-1160835.html.

- Punctuality: One of the classic German virtues, surpassed at best by its Swiss neighbors.

- Aloofness: Germans can seem a bit reserved and cool at first. Sometimes they lack cordiality.

- Lack of humor: Joie de vivre as in Southern Europe or South America is often uncommon for Germans. A certain sobriety and seriousness prevails in business life.

- Correctness: Germans are considered to be very reliable.

- Historical awareness: Due to the Nazi era and the two world wars, a culture of not forgetting is deeply rooted in the horrors of the past.

- Love for rules: From rules for waste separation to bureaucratic structures and the most comprehensive tax legislation in the world, this reverence for rules occasionally hinders pragmatism and innovation.

- Directness: Germans are not terribly fond of small talk and prefer to get straight to the point. In business meetings, for example, people prefer an objective and goal-oriented discussion.[31]

IMPACT OF LSP IN THE CONTEXT OF GERMAN STEREOTYPES

Clichés are characterized by the fact that they only show one side of the coin and often only provide a superficial description. The world is not just black or white. Yet behind every cliché there is also a spark of truth. But how can LSP be of lasting benefit to those German behavior patterns identified as conspicuous? Below are a few examples:

- Germans keep their distance: LSP can easily help to get a deeper understanding of the personalities in any given team.

- Germans are joyless: LSP is able to bring a certain lightness into working sessions that are otherwise characterized by rationality. This promotes concentration, the involvement of all participants, creativity, and enables joy of working.

- Germans and their bureaucracy: LSP can help to question established systems and procedures as well as unleash creativity.

- Germans tend to be direct and overly critical: LSP can help to externalize conflicting situations. The personal direct approach (from which, for example, introverted Germans also suffer from) is weakened and ensures a better working atmosphere.

---

[31] "Interesting Facts about Germans You Never Knew.," Club GLOBALS, May 28, 2018, https://clubglobals.com/interesting-facts-about-germans/.

Creativity-supporting business design tools have become very popular in Germany. Today, many well-known corporations and medium-sized companies use tools such as design thinking, the Business Model Canvas, and LEGO® SERIOUS PLAY®. In the German-language social network XING, more than 700 professionals have indicated they are providers of services related to LSP.

Experience in recent years has also shown that LSP has become very popular, particularly among the engineering professions, which are strongly represented in Germany. The haptic nature and the hands-on thinking that underlies the method is very popular among this strongly male-dominated professional group. The common fields of application of the method, from short impulse workshops and coaching to systemic analysis and strategy work, are all being practiced in Germany.

Nevertheless, there are still many skeptics whose rational mindsets prevent them from being able to appreciate any form of serious play in a business context. In such cases, success requires introducing LSP in demo workshops or sharing best practice use cases. It must be noted that the increased knowledge about and acceptance of LSP over recent years has proved beneficial in real-world situations, as the following case study illustrates.

■ CASE STUDY: LEGO® SERIOUS PLAY® & CONFLICT MANAGEMENT OR EAST VERSUS WEST GERMANY ■

In addition to the previously described clichés about Germans, within our relatively small country there are behaviors specifically attributed to different regions. Northern Germans, for example, are occasionally described as being cool and reserved, while the Swabians in Southern Germany are extremely frugal. In the context of our recent history (keyword reunification), there are also reservations and clichés between people who lived and still live in the former East versus those in West Germany. Recently, these cultural differences prompted a company to hold a workshop with LSP.

Background

The CEO of a medium-sized mechanical engineering company with several plants in different areas of Germany participated in a design thinking conference. During a short breakout session, he got his first introduction to LSP. Inspired by this session, he initiated a workshop on conflict management between two departments: Sales in West Germany and Supply Chain Management in East Germany

Project Briefing

The briefing explained that employees in the East had all worked with a predecessor company at the site during GDR (German Democratic Republic) times. The people there are used to starting work very early in the morning, at around 6.30 a.m., and going home at 3 p.m. at the latest. Employees in the West, on the other hand, start their working day at around 9 a.m. and often do not finish until after 6 p.m. This meant the sales employees could never reach any colleague in the East after 3 p.m. This was problematic when they needed to initiate important and time-sensitive orders. Each group was also strongly influenced by silo thinking. In short, the two departments needed to work together but did not appreciate each other because of their different work styles and attitudes. The CEO's drastic observation was, "They hate each other." The teams had already previously engaged in a variety of unsuccessful mediation and teambuilding initiatives.

Objective

Inspired by the earlier LSP Workshop, the company CEO hoped the playful approach of LSP could help to eliminate the conflict that had been smoldering for some time. He had three specific goals. The first was to improve understanding between the two departments. He also wanted them to utilize 3D thinking to visualize a target picture of their smooth cooperation in the near future. Finally, they needed to draw up an action plan.

Setting

We planned a two-day event at an ideally located business hotel, directly at the former border on neutral territory. The event was to start with a total of eight executives, four from each department, but without the CEO.

Prelude

The atmosphere in the room was very reserved at the beginning of the event, but it gradually improved with the deployment of LSP. They broke the ice during skills building, when I asked them to build the worst-assumed boss. This common image of the enemy caused some laughter at first.

INTERMEDIATE PHASE

Because the two departments were in a kind of internal customer relationship with each other, I planned an intermediate phase after the skills building to focus on problematic customer relationships. I tasked the participants with building a specific experience from their private sphere to show how they themselves, as customers, were once extremely dissatisfied. As they shared their stories, I briefly noted the cause of each person's dissatisfaction and their expected reaction from the other person. We also speculated about why the respective service provider had performed poorly. This intermediate step proved to be extremely helpful, because the participants were able to build up empathy.

SITUATION ANALYSIS

In the next step, we conducted an analysis of the company's situation. I asked the participants to build a specific story with LSP, depicting an experience in which they were very annoyed with the other department. Before they shared their stories, I emphasized the LEGO etiquette once again: No objections, just questions about the model, etc.

We listened to each story in turn and visualized the main points on the flipchart: What happened and what reaction would you have expected from the other person? After hearing everyone's experiences, we reflected in detail from a meta-level. The participants quickly worked out that their cultural differences were not the most obvious problem. LSP brought the core of the conflicts to light: Both units were evaluated on the basis of contradictory key-performance-indicators. Among other things, sales were measured in terms of short customer response times and customer satisfaction. Supply chain management was measured in terms of short storage times and costs.

TEAM IDENTITY

For further mutual understanding, both departments separately built their departmental identity as a shared model with a systemic representation of the main actors and stakeholders. A certified LSP facilitator was present at each table, a co-moderator helped to carry out this time-consuming step. The teams presented their systems to each other. And in our final discussion of the day, we visualized and recorded their new findings. They identified even more issues, such as the lack of communication between managers, which caused the silo thinking mentality to persist.

▰▰ VISION ▰▰▰▰▰▰▰▰▰▰▰▰▰▰▰▰▰▰▰▰▰▰▰▰▰▰▰▰▰▰▰▰

On the second day, the participants used LSP to construct an ideal picture of the teams' future cooperation. They began with individual models, and then created a shared model with the essential elements from the individual models. They occasionally took into account some of the cultural differences they had previously identified, but those mostly seemed irrelevant at this point. They came to some solid agreements, one being the team in the East would be available for contact until 5 p.m.

▰▰ ACTION PLAN ▰▰▰▰▰▰▰▰▰▰▰▰▰▰▰▰▰▰▰▰▰▰▰▰▰▰▰▰

The teams developed an action plan, with fixed responsibilities and deadlines.

▰▰ CONCLUSION ▰▰▰▰▰▰▰▰▰▰▰▰▰▰▰▰▰▰▰▰▰▰▰▰▰▰▰▰

At the end of the session, the participants reflected a high level of satisfaction with the workshop's results. The participants also commented extremely positively on the workshop design they had just experienced with the LSP Method.

▰▰ FOLLOW UP ▰▰▰▰▰▰▰▰▰▰▰▰▰▰▰▰▰▰▰▰▰▰▰▰▰▰▰▰▰▰▰

I provided the workshop report as a PowerPoint presentation with linked video recordings. During the workshop, we used the app "JustPressRecord," which immediately transcribes verbal recordings (available in various languages) into text modules.

▰▰ UNCOVERING THE HIDDEN LAYERS ▰▰▰▰▰▰▰▰▰▰▰▰▰▰▰▰

Stereotypes about the people of different regions can sometimes be helpful in understanding differences. These clichés exist and often also characterize a culture to a certain extent. In the context of business challenges, however, these are often only the outer shell of a problem. As the case study illustrates, LSP is particularly good at identifying the true core of a challenging situation.

Regarding the general application of LSP in Germany, it can be noted the underlying advantages of the method (e.g. in-depth discussions, diversity of thought, the inclusion of all users, and in particular the fun factor) are able to neutralize some of the more negative stereotypes.

7

MEXICO: PLAYING TO IMPROVE TEAM DYNAMICS

By Hugo Alvarado

I confess that at first, I was skeptical about the usefulness of the LEGO® SERIOUS PLAY® methodology. I thought it was a joke, and this was because my first experience with it was very bad. Consequently, I denied myself the opportunity to know it in depth for some time. However, I gave it a second chance and learned I had been wrong. I want to share with you how I went from being a skeptic to a practitioner who has been able to collaborate with Mexican companies and people as well, in order to achieve impressive results.

As a facilitator, business consultant, and coach, I have always tried to be up on the state of the art of business methodologies. I began my career as a Computer Science Engineer, holding master's degrees in business management and marketing. I also worked 20 years as a business advisor, which included eight years at Ernst & Young México. This provided me with proven and widely accepted analytical and methodological elements to reach desired results. Because of this background, when I first learned about the LEGO® SERIOUS PLAY® methodology I thought it sounded pretty weird. My structured mind did not allow me to see how, through serious play, I could help participants to reach deep results and conclusions. Who would have thought I would become not only a practitioner and promoter of this methodology, but also a trainer of it?

I want to share with you how this transformation happened, and how I discovered LSP's applications. I will explain how I had to adapt LEGO® SERIOUS PLAY® to not only the Mexican culture, but also to that of specific organizations. Finally, I will list some of the transitional benefits of the transformations I have witnessed through my LSP interventions.

▬ FIRST STEPS ▬

After my first unsuccessful experience, I began to take note of some LinkedIn posts from a colleague who was utilizing LEGO® SERIOUS PLAY®. Initially, I thought about hiring a certified facilitator to design and facilitate my workshops, but then I realized that not knowing the methodology would make it harder for me to see the whole picture. A simple question like, "What is the goal you want as a result of the workshop?" would be very difficult for me to answer satisfactorily.

I began to evaluate the option of becoming certified, but the required investment in time, money, and effort raised many doubts in my mind: What will it do me? How will I get advantage of it? What if it does not work for me? Will I have wasted my savings? What if it is a scam? What if it is only for people with background in psychology or something similar? Curiously, I could not find the answers to my questions in Mexico. I did, however, find them within Strategic Play. At the time they did not have representation in Mexico, but they did in San Diego. With the knowledge that winning requires risk, I decided to take the training.

During the training days, my mind did not stop spinning. Each exercise was accompanied by ideas of how I could apply LEGO® SERIOUS PLAY® in my workshops. I began to have so many ideas, I dedicated a couple hours at the end of each day to write them all down and trying to give them a logical order. At the end of the training, I asked myself the question every facilitator has when receiving their certificate: What is next?

I already had traditional workshops about consultative selling as well as business model and value proposition design. Upon my return to Mexico, I decided to start converting these to the LEGO® SERIOUS PLAY® methodology so I could offer them to my clients, prospects, and allies. While I considered my results good, there was also a lot of learning. I felt my first workshops succeeded in engaging the audience, but I was not sure if they generated the full impact I expected. I also learned you do not simply convert workshops to LSP. To get the most from a session, you need to redesign it with a completely new approach. So I started the exciting journey of reinventing my own offerings and value propositions.

I learned a lot during the rediscovery of my own needs and those of my clients. I found a wide variety of issues impacting Mexican organizations, specifically relating to team dynamics. Here are just three from a very long list.

▬▬ A MATTER OF TRUST AND EMPATHY ▬▬▬▬▬▬▬

In my work with Mexican organizations, I often find that during meetings, workshops, or teambuilding sessions, participants find it hard to share what they really mean. They struggle to find the right words. They prefer to wait for another person to share before them, if they share at all. On the other side, people who believe they have been referenced feel attacked or offended. In short, Mexicans find it difficult to share what they really think with their peers or their bosses. As a result, there are a lot of meetings in which we talk about many things but not the main issues. Furthermore, we Mexicans tend to be very good at speaking but not so much at listening. This makes it hard for us to understand others' points of view.

I will illustrate this with two recent cases in which I was invited to participate. In the first one, a major national retail chain hired me to execute a team-building workshop for the personnel within its Human Resources department. There were around 80 people who, despite being in the same department, were physically distributed between two buildings located 10 minutes away from each other. This made it difficult for team members to communicate, collaborate, and integrate. The objective of the workshop was to identify barriers and bridges to improve communication.

In a 3-hour workshop, using the 3D Diagnostic Cards and the Exploration Bags, participants were able to identify the main communication barriers, including: I do not know him/her; I think he/she is very young or old; I do not know what he/she does; I am afraid of asking and sounding silly, etc. Additionally, there was a great generational gap between senior employees and the most recent hires. Many attendees were surprised to learn they shared similar fears. Managers were able to observe differences and similarities between sub-areas. They focused more on the message rather than on the messenger, and they understood it was not personal. When moving to the stage where they had to discover and define communications bridges, the participants became optimistic because the LEGO® SERIOUS PLAY® activities allowed them to collaboratively design creative solutions. First, they found the low hanging fruits. Then they started to build more complex solutions on the ideas of others. The final models turned out to be very creative and widely accepted by all.

Another example was with a major company in the textile industry, where it was very difficult for participants from operations, logistics, and sales to feel accountable. They also found it difficult to agree and collaborate with a customer-centric mindset. It was very common for them maintain their position, while holding other areas accountable for failures and delays in the delivery time. I planned and executed various team-building and process improvement workshops with LEGO® SERIOUS PLAY®, which included activities where they had to build three-dimensional models in order to discover that their point of view is just that—a single point of view. By literally changing places, they could see another perspective. I also carried out activities to understand the challenges each one faces, so they could understand everything is within a cause and effect chain. As a result, they got more empathetic and willing to understand each other's points of view, generating optimal emotional states of mind in order to understand the challenges of their counterparts. Finally, I also carried out activities to promote the feeling of shared achievement by celebrating small successes, which in turn led to the success of the group. And it is precisely these feelings of continuous achievement that encouraged them to search for new mechanisms of effective communication so they could achieve their objectives as a team. They build the result. It was not imposed by an internal or external agent, so they were able to avoid frustration and resistance to change.

THE RODEO AND THE TIP OF THE ICEBERG

If there is something that characterizes us, it is the large number of words we can say per minute. For some people, this causes them to take longer getting to their main point. In traditional meetings, this can allow some participants to use up all the time while others remain silent without getting the chance to say anything. This often leads to confusing the problems with their effects, which can make it difficult for us to find the root cause of an issue.

During a strategic thinking and risk analysis project I executed for a Mexican insurance broker, I started with a diagnostic phase that included interviews and focus groups with the staff from the areas of sales, risks, customer service, and claims, among others. Using individual LEGO® SERIOUS PLAY® models, in combination with the 3D Diagnostic Cards, participants were able to build stories representing a cause and effect analysis. Thanks to the ground rules we established at the

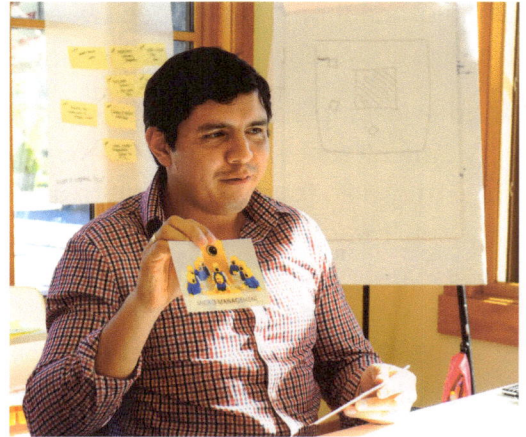

beginning, participants had equal time to participate and were motivated to be concrete and stay focused. As a result, they were able to reflect on how they felt and about what was happening within the company, resulting from the fact no one was questioning the actions of others or company policies and procedures. For the execution phase of the workshops, we were able to get the participants to focus and be more concrete and direct in their contributions. This was thanks to the three-dimensional models based on LEGO® SERIOUS PLAY® that they built, both individually and in a shared way. This allowed for rapid consensus building regarding the future desired state and the main actions to follow.

■ THE BIG PICTURE AND THE WHAT IFS ■

We are optimists. We expect things are going to turn out well, and we don't like it when someone tells us what can happen. This has its advantages, allowing us to work proactively to achieve our objectives, trusting there will always be a strong wind. But the reality is, we must also consider potential risks; it is often difficult for us to see the whole picture.

This happened in a major Human Resources management company where I facilitated several strategy and risk analysis workshops. It was a family business that grew up very quickly in a very short period of time, and it lacked standardized processes, policies, and best practices. The founding partners handled all decisions and authorizations; and in that moment, they wanted to prepare the succession to the next generation. An issue that came up in the diagnosis is something very common within Mexican family businesses: It was very difficult for employees to make decisions without consulting the partners, mainly because they had been conditioned to behave in that way. My job was to design, implement, and automate their main business processes and also to execute a change management plan. I started by analyzing the current situation, applying LEGO® SERIOUS PLAY® and 3D Diagnostic Cards, which yielded enough material to carry out workshops for strategic thinking and risk analysis. The activities with LSP allowed the partners to see the big picture of the organization and to rethink their business practices that had worked in a particular moment. Now these same practices were precisely what was holding back their growth and forcing them to continue working in the business.

By designing their future state using LEGO® SERIOUS PLAY®, they were able to visualize it, define the steps to get there, and also identify potential risks that could prevent them from reaching their goal. With LEGO® SERIOUS PLAY®, they were able to create risk scenarios and evaluate their impact in their business in such a positive way, they proactively defined actions to prepare for and even possibly prevent the scenarios from materializing. They were open to discussing difficult issues, while finding solutions to anticipate and reduce the risk of occurrence and impact. In fact, the results were so positive they proved useful during the health crisis derived from COVID-19, in which they launched their processes and contingency plans.

▬ GOING ONLINE ▬

Before COVID-19, I never thought the online delivery of LSP workshops was a possibility. Everyone believed it was something that could only work in person. But the crisis brought on by this virus taught us otherwise. As the situation unfolded, we saw an opportunity to expand the possibilities of LEGO® SERIOUS PLAY®.

Everything started when Jacqueline Lloyd Smith (our founder) worked alongside Maxine King (our curriculum developer) and Stephen James Walling (our training coach) to design the online LEGO® SERIOUS PLAY® training. I facilitated the first online training in Mexico to participants who registered for in-person training prior to the arrival of COVID-19. There were many challenges, and we understood this would be a completely different experience from our previous offerings. We had many new logistical issues to consider, including delivery of materials and a variety of technical aspects to ensure a smooth experience for both facilitators and learners. This was a major undertaking and I wish to share a summary of my insights.

One of the early online workshops I offered was for a large bank in Mexico, specializing in microcredit for small business owners and entrepreneurs. The team members lived in Mexico City and State of Mexico, Mexico. The workshop was 10-hours long. Objectives included helping the participants to get to know each other on a more personal level, promoting greater unity amongst the team, and letting them identify key challenges, such as satisfying internal clients. The session included a root cause analysis using the 3D Diagnostic cards, as well as activities to find the strengths, aspirations, and requirements of each team member. The participants also had the opportunity to build a shared model representing the characteristics of a high-performance team and their simple guiding principles.

Right now, as I write this chapter, I am delivering a series of workshops related to strategy and change management for a large company that is going through a process of becoming more institutionalized and passing from the first generation (founders) to the second generation (the founders' daughters). This is a two-years project that started in 2020 with in person LEGO® SERIOUS PLAY® workshops related to strategic planning and has continued in 2021 with change management workshops. So participants have been exposed to and have had the opportunity to experience both in-person and online workshops. The participants have commented they would rather be doing in-person sessions; but considering the circumstances, they would rather have the workshops online rather than replace them with other activities or postpone the workshops.

Going online has allowed Mexican companies with offices around the world to expand their reach. It has also given me the opportunity to learn several things I now consider to be key success factors:

1   The power of LEGO® SERIOUS PLAY® can be delivered online and opens the opportunity for dispersed teams to take advantage of this methodology, as long as it is thoughtfully and correctly facilitated using the same underpinnings developed by LEGO®.

2   The experience of online vs. in-person workshops has to be designed differently; it is not just a matter of technology.

3   The logistics involved in the online workshops imply new challenges, including the distribution of materials and planning the agenda while taking into account different time zones in Mexico.

4   Online workshops can be segmented into small modules, and these can be carried out on different days or weeks. This enriches the participants' experience because they then engage in tasks and activities in between sessions. In face-to-face workshops, this all occurs within a few consecutive days.

5   I viewed technology as an enabler rather than an obstacle.

6   I always have backup plans for a variety of scenarios, which include a co-facilitator for support and an alternate location in case of Internet or electrical failures.

7   I work to keep the teams small for each facilitator. In the case of online workshops, teams of six people per facilitator seem to be ideal.

8   I include activities to allow participants some physical movement as well as breaks from screen time.

9   The final deliverable becomes even more relevant online in order to summarize the learnings and agreements of the workshop.

CONCLUSIONS

From my personal experience, LEGO® SERIOUS PLAY® is a very powerful methodology. You must, however, have adequate preparation and experience to carry it out. Otherwise, your participants may have a negative experience and lose intertest in LSP just as I did. It may seem simple, but it is not. It is not just about integrating activities within your workshops so participants can play with LEGO® bricks, giving them the feeling of play. LEGO® SERIOUS PLAY® can be a very powerful tool that leads to extraordinary results.

LEGO® SERIOUS PLAY® applications are diverse and can have different impacts. It is important to take into consideration the context, the culture, the organization, and the team.

As a summary, in this chapter we have observed how LSP has been useful in Mexican organizations to:

- Build trust among team members: peers, bosses and subordinates.
- Achieve openness in people and accept other's ideas.
- Visualize various perspectives and points of view.
- Encourage empathy, putting yourself in someone else's shoes, and achieve harmony by being on the same communication channel to achieve active listening.
- Handle deep problems within team dynamics, taking care of the relationship between team members.
- Achieve focus and synthesis on the ideas from the participants, maximizing the time dedicated to meetings, workshops, or integration sessions.
- Deepen the analysis of problems, separating the symptoms from the root causes, and promoting critical thinking both individually and in groups.

- Generate optimal states of minds in order to search for solutions.
- Visualize the big picture of a situation, idea, concept, or circumstance, integrating the diverse points of view and unifying them in consensual models.
- Raise awareness about the risk situations to which businesses are exposed and to creatively think about solutions should issues materialize.

We have also seen that LEGO® SERIOUS PLAY® can be delivered online in Mexico, but the experience requires a new design to provide the best experience for the participants. It also has it owns challenges in terms of logistics, tools, and delivery.

8

PANAMA: LEARNING THROUGH PLAY IN A TRADITIONAL CULTURE

Jihan Rodríguez ©

By Rosa Mon

My name is Rosa Mon, and I am Panamanian. My passion for teaching and facilitating is a family heritage. I come from a large family where my grandparents instilled in us that we must always help others, but the condition was to do so by helping them to develop their potential. That way they could not only help themselves, but they could also positively impact others. This is why I decided to study psychology and specialize with a master's degree in education.

In my professional life, I have always worked in the area of human development. I have gone from hospitality and customer service to senior management and sports, and from the field of private business and personal development to government projects at the national level. In this journey of more than 20 years, I have managed to train over 10,000 people. I have also worked with more than 200 professional athletes, impacting them in a positive way and with extraordinary results.

I am always looking for tools and methods that stimulate creativity and effectively transmit or generate knowledge. That is why I have been part of the StrategicPlay community for over 10 years. The methodologies have been a great asset in my work in Latin America, helping me to get the best out of each team and person I help.

BUILDING AND DISCOVERING DEEP HUMAN STORIES

My discovery of LEGO® SERIOUS PLAY® begins with what I call the Journey of the Millennium Falcon. In 2006, I decided to become a business entrepreneur and dedicated myself to training companies on issues of customer service and talent development. I teamed up with my husband Jaime in this venture, and ever since we have been looking for the best tools to help develop those soft skills every human being needs to be a great leader.

Jaime is a big Star Wars fan. In November 2010, while searching for gifts for our son and nephews, he noticed the local toy shops were carrying LEGO® Star Wars sets again. These had practically disappeared from the Latin American market in the 2000s. There is one particular set he always dreamed of but never had the chance to own: the LEGO® Millennium Falcon. That particular box did not arrive in Panama that Christmas, so he began a search online to see if he could order it. He spent so much time looking for it, I asked him, "Why do you like LEGO so much?" He replied, "LEGO is the eternal toy. If it breaks, you can put it back together; and if you get bored of the model, you can take it apart and build something new. If you lose a piece, you can take one from another model and you are building something new."

I became curious: Was there any educational tool with those same benefits? My husband and I searched, and the first thing we found was LEGO® Education. It had spectacular sets, but they focused more on children and adolescents. At the time, those sets would not work for me because I was working more with adults and professionals. But we kept looking and asking around, and the search paid off when we discovered LEGO® SERIOUS PLAY®.

We immediately read the LEGO® SERIOUS PLAY® Open Source document. Although it only describes the most basic ways of using the tool, we realized its potential. We began checking out LEGO® SERIOUS PLAY® professional communities, writing to all the Master Trainers we could find. We hoped to find someone who would be interested in coming to Panama to train us. We spent two days checking our email every 10 minutes, hoping for a response. Finally, it happened: We got an email from Jacqueline Lloyds Smith of Strategic Play Canada. She wrote to find out more about us and our needs. We told her about our work and what we wanted to achieve with the tool. She explained more about its use and how it could help with talent development. After a couple of emails and phone conversations, we

were convinced we needed to train our entire team in the LSP methodology. It was something we had never seen in Central America and Panama, despite much talk about creativity and innovation in the region.

In September 2011, we finally got to take the LSP methodology certification training in Panama. After we participated in the training, we were surprised by the impact of the methodology. Days later, we could still clearly remember the models we built, the ideas we shared, and the conclusions we reached.

This training far exceeded our expectations, and we were excited to learn about the many ways we could use the methodology. We quickly decided to make Panamanian companies aware of the benefits their people and teams could receive. We could use LSP to help them develop their talent, solve complex prob-lems, have more effective communication, generate ideas, make quick decisions, and raise their performance to the highest level.

We were convinced the potential of the method had to be experienced. Explaining through conversation or marketing would not be effective. So we prepared a launch event at the Marriott Hotel in downtown Panama City. We invited leaders from a variety of industries: banking, education, hotels and tourism, transporta-tion, logistics, and sports. We asked them to join us to learn about our company, and more specifically to give LSP a try. We originally planned for 50 participants, but the event generated so much interest we hit 100 registrants.

On the big day, we began with live music on the guitar from Stephen Walling. While live music is common at social functions, it is not something people expect at a training event. Following the music, we heard a presentation from Carlos Rabat Mallol, a local businessman and community leader. He discussed the importance of innovation and looking outside Panama to bring back the best new trends to the region that would ultimately create new opportunities.

We had worried people would not attend because rain was predicted; however, approximately 115 people arrived at the launch event. Once people got their hands on the bricks, they spontaneously shared their tower stories and used them to network with complete strangers. This event gave us the chance for people to hear, see, and experience for themselves the value of LSP. We hired a professional photographer to take photos to use in our marketing materials. We also brought in a professional translator and had the entire event simultaneously translated in English and Spanish. After a few activities with the bricks, we served small plates of food. Everyone stayed to eat and network instead of trying to drive home in the rain and heavy, slow-moving traffic. The feedback we received was interesting. Most of the participants found they could apply the methodology to solve problems in their work areas. Some even thought of using it at the individual level, in personalized coaching.

LEGO® SERIOUS PLAY® represented a real solution for us. In a very short time, we could go from identifying a problem to finding concrete actions to start solving it. This tool would be of great value to the companies in our region.

Within the first 30 minutes of the launch, we saw the magic of the hand-brain connection: An association hired us to carry out our first LSP methods workshop. They wanted us to work with a team of entrepreneurs, consultants, managers, and executive coaches from various companies, who were seeking strategies to achieve their goals. The unique way this tool combines visual, auditory, and kinesthetic learning styles allows people to literally lend a hand to their brain. There was a powerful learning moment everyone got to observe, involving a man who had been trying for years to achieve his goal. As he was explaining his model to the group, he suddenly discovered the obstacle that had been standing in his way. Even more amazing was to observe how, just by changing the position of a LEGO® brick, he managed to unlock his ideas, actions, and emotional state in a positive way.

Another thing that surprised us was the way LSP depersonalizes ideas and problems. In a typical meeting, people develop an association between an idea and the person who contributed it. If the individual does not project security, trust, or leadership, it is very likely the others will discard the idea immediately. But the advantage with LEGO® SERIOUS PLAY® is that everyone discusses the ideas represented by the 3D models; they do not have a discussion about the builders. Furthermore, everyone has the same level of participation, which allows for a much more objective analysis of ideas. In a culture like Panama's, where appearance and authority greatly influence the decision-making in organizations, this methodology gives voice to those who are marginalized but have much to contribute.

■■■ THE VERSATILITY OF LSP ■■■■■■■■■■■■■■■■■

To emphasize how truly versatile this method is, here is a surprising success story. We used LSP while working with "NOSSA VITORIA," the women's team of the open category of paddle cayuco. The team went on to achieve an extraordinary record, which they still maintain today. Panama is the only country in the world where native cayuco racing is a sport. The United States military developed this sports competition during the years they worked at the military bases that controlled the Panama Canal. They learned to use the cayuco rowing boats of the natives of the area and created a competitive sport as a way to integrate with the culture of the

country. The race consists of rowing from the Atlantic Ocean to the Pacific Ocean, passing through the locks of the Panama Canal. The "NOSSA VITORIA" team won the race in 2014 and 2015. So they set out to be the first women's team to win the three-time championship.

The team was doing very well, and they wondered how they could accomplish the seemingly impossible: They needed to take their bodies and performance to even more extreme limits. This is where we came to the rescue with LSP. The team engaged in strategic planning by building a 3D model, which connected all the physical, technical, strategic, mental, and emotional aspects necessary to compete in an extreme state. This helped the team to become better aligned, enhance their strengths, establish actions they could take to deal with potential obstacles, develop strategies to transform their weaknesses into their hidden power, and to identify ways to remain calm in difficult moments, allowing their inner strength to drive their best performance. Using LSP allowed everyone to actively participate while thinking creatively, planning their race together in a fun way. Their hard work paid off. The "NOSSA VITORIA" team was able to reach new records and become champions in 2016. They are the only women's three-time champions to date.

THE UNEXPECTED

Not all experiences are good, of course. But even the bad experiences can offer valuable learning. After we began LSP training, we encountered some difficulties we had not anticipated. Going in, we knew LSP materials are expensive. But we quickly discovered there is no direct distribution to Panama and Central America, making it very complex and costly just to acquire the materials.

On one occasion, we were invited to an annual executives' convention to demonstrate creative coaching with the LSP Methodology with 100 people. Despite our best efforts to emphasize that we needed the LEGO® bricks returned to us after the demonstration, we only got half of the sets back. At first, we were amused to see people getting up, pretending to answer a phone call or visit the bathroom while secreting away the LEGO bricks in their bags or pockets. It was like watching children saving candy after breaking a piñata at a party. Unfortunately, this represented a significant material and economic loss for our team. After this, our event budgets included the cost to replace some or all of the materials. LEGO bricks generate a personal and emotional connection. They bring back happy childhood memories, people want to share them with their children, and they want to bring home the ideas they created in their model. That is why people are so tempted to take the LEGO with them.

PANAMA AND CENTRAL AMERICA: THE CHALLENGES USING LSP

Many organizations talk about improving their results through the use of creativity and innovation. But our culture is still very traditional, and people only see LEGO® bricks as children's toys. As a result, people are very skeptical about the effectiveness and cost-benefit value of LSP. In addition, it makes the sales very complex. Sales are not limited to sending an email or brochure, or making a phone call. It requires a presentation with a short demonstration, allowing the decision-makers to discover the tool's potential. Many companies do not have the necessary time frames to allow for this. Another challenge we often face is the amount of time companies are willing to make available for the workshops. They envision a group dynamic that will take 10 – 30 minutes. But an LSP process can take at least four hours, depending on the scope we must achieve.

The other significant challenge for our region is what we call *imitation competitors*. They are people who falsely claim to be certified, and then carry out activities in companies and businesses with predictably bad results. This can discredit brands and sometimes even entire industries. This happens in our region regularly, and not just with LSP. It has happened in design thinking and with project managers and coaches. These people participate in a single workshop and then pose as experts. This is why it is so important to verify you are hiring facilitators or trainers who are certified with institutions or companies that endorse worldwide.

LSP MODIFICATIONS FOR CULTURAL EFFECTIVENESS

The LSP methodology works perfectly with a variety of cultures, and it does not require people to have any experience building with LEGO. On one occasion, we held a workshop with doctors from Cuba. Only one of the participants knew what LEGO was, but they had never built with it before. It was impressive to see the building techniques with this unfamiliar material. Not only did the methodology flow perfectly, but the doctors found creative new ways to make connections. They used the bricks in ways we had never seen in our previous workshops.

While anyone can build with LEGO, we have made some minor adaptations to how we use the LSP methodology to better fit in our culture. For example, there is an activity in the Starter Kit where participants build animals to demonstrate the value of metaphors. The suggested animals are not native to our region, so we use animals that will better relate to our audiences. We will substitute turtles for walruses and chickens for ostriches. There is another activity, where people are tasked with building a go kart to demonstrate process and key points of innovation. We found that many of the participants we work with are unfamiliar with go karts, so we ask everyone to build a car or a boat instead.

We also sometimes add pieces to kits. When clients request workshops or activities, we must identify the appropriate kit to use according to their objectives, number of participants, and type of audience. We find we can help people to better represent their ideas or to achieve greater meaning in their stories by adding relevant pieces. For example, when we worked with the cayuco team, we included a LEGO canoe from a non-LSP set. And with Minifigures, we add accessories and heads with different facial expressions. In our region, people are very expressive with nonverbal language. There is also a great multiracial variety in our region, so we like to use a variety of colors in Minifigure parts. So while we do make some cosmetic changes to help people express themselves more easily, the methodology remains the same.

BUILDING A BRIDGE TO THE FUTURE

Over time, we have noticed a greater acceptance of the LSP methodology among the younger generations in Panama and Central America. They maintain an open mind and look beyond tradition in their constant search for innovation, new methods, practical tools, and technology. The new generations do not want to settle for meaningless jobs. They want careers that are both fun and fulfilling.

Due to globalization, people can be affected by events happening anywhere in the world. Radical changes are constantly occurring in many areas, including climate, technology, medicine, and negotiations between countries. As these changes occur, people and organizations must be able to react quickly to adapt and function as new situations arise. Utilizing LEGO® SERIOUS PLAY® will prove to be highly beneficial. Regardless of the circumstance, LSP strategy sessions are effective for defining challenges and discovering actions to help move forward in the face of difficulties.

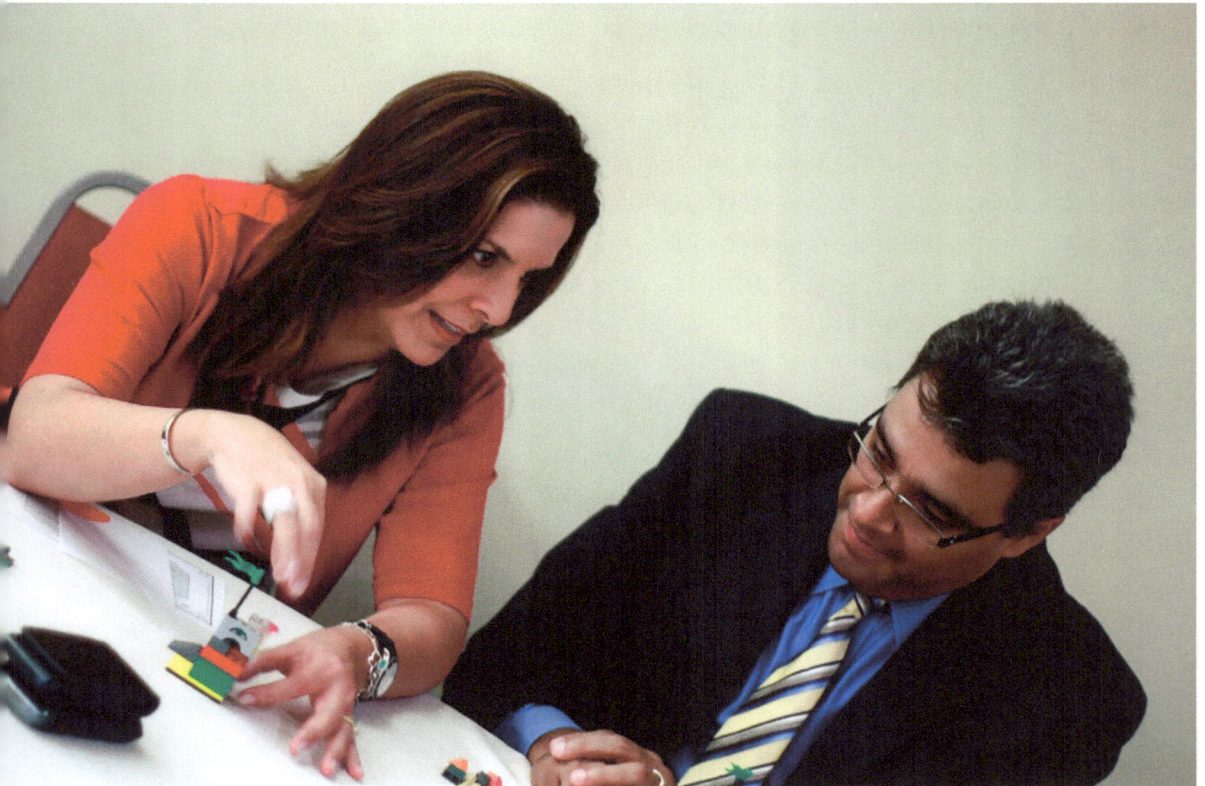

9

SPAIN: BROADENING THE DEFINITION OF CREATIVITY

By Arturo Giménez

The ability of maps to tell stories is fascinating. Since the beginning of time, cartography has been, and continues to be, a key element in the evolution of humanity. Discoveries, wars, peace processes, and all developments of a social, economic, or cultural nature, have always had a significant impact on maps. Historically, European maps have always placed this continent in the center of the world. In 1884, the International Meridian Conference was held in Washington D.C. Here it was agreed the meridian passing through the English town of Greenwich would be adopted as the reference from which Earth longitude is measured—meridian 0.

Some of the most influential civilizations originated in Europe. We had ancient Greece, the cradle of democracy, and the many innovations of ancient Rome. Major historical events occurred in Europe, such as the Industrial and French revolutions, the rise of communism, and the two world wars. Therefore, in addition to geography we must also acknowledge the role of history in Europe's direct influences on the rest of the world.

My name is Arturo Giménez and I was born in Valencia, Spain. As far as I know, we all must come into this world somewhere. I did not choose it, so I saw the light in that city. Throughout my life I have had the opportunity to work and get to know a

large number of countries, including all of Latin America. I have always believed that anyone from Spain should visit and learn about at least one Latin American country. Only in this way can one discover the true dimension of the bonds that unite us on both sides of the Atlantic. As well, I recommend anyone born in Latin America to visit Spain. From that mutual knowledge, we could bury many of the prejudices that exist within our community. In this chapter, I seek to provide insights into my observations of how creativity is woven into the culture of Spain, and also why LSP is so useful when people are open to accepting that which is new.

Spain has been a relevant actor in the history of Europe and the world as we know it today. Considering the two variables mentioned above, it has been and is a bridge between Africa and Europe, sender and receiver of citizens to and from the entire American continent, and a country where millions of Europeans have chosen to reside. Spain is also the second most visited country in the world. The Spanish language is spoken by more than 500 million people around the world. And in the United States, it is the second most used language after English.

At this point, it is not easy to put a label on Spain. Is it a traditional country, attached to its history, customs, and habits? Or is it a cosmopolitan, advanced, and avant-garde country? Perhaps the best answer is that Spain is both very diverse and complex. There are many realities within it, and it is not exempt from territorial tensions. Sometimes these tensions are dramatic, as in the case of the years of terrorism. Others use more democratic channels, such as elections.

The country has an important variety of official languages in addition to Spanish. There is a wide range of climatic zones, from the desert areas of the Canary Islands to the high mountain climate, to the mild Mediterranean. Spain has a pronounced orography, having the continent's second highest average altitude after Switzerland. Spain also has a host of cultural peculiarities. A person born and raised in the rural interior of Galicia, in the North, will see a person born in the cosmopolitan city of Barcelona as a true alien, and vice versa.

We are therefore faced with a piece of land where millions of people of different cultures, religions, and origins coexist. Spain has wealthy retirees from Northern Europe, immigrants from south of the Sahara, and Latin American families living alongside many others from Eastern Europe. This creates a melting pot of realities in Spain, which has only served to enrich the country. And this follows the first settlements of the Lower Paleolithic in 800,000 BC, which witnessed the passage and settlement of Phoenicians, Greeks, Romans, Carthaginians, Celts, Iberians, Visigoths, Muslims, and Christians.

Here, the word tradition acquires important connotations. Beyond the superficiality of a large part of our routines, there is a residue of uses, customs, and traditions that has to do with episodes and situations that happened centuries ago. These remain, to a degree, in the subconscious of the population. Spain is a country grounded in an extraordinarily significant past but one that also offers significant diversity in many areas.

What does all this analysis have to do with a method like LEGO® SERIOUS PLAY®? Where is the point of synergy between an openly creative, effective, and powerful methodology and a diverse, yet traditional nation? The best way to explain it is with a real-life example and by exploring creativity in Spain.

CREATIVITY IN SPAIN

Culturally speaking, Spain is a country with a very specific image of the concept of creativity. Of course, it is well seen and accepted; however, that only happens in specific areas. How can a country that has Picasso, Gaudí, Cervantes, or Dalí as world references deny the idea of creativity? This is a country where gastronomy is a party and flamenco is a sign of world identity and even sport. Yet this only limits the field of action of creativity. That is, in the social subconscious, creativity is well accepted as long as it remains in the traditional realm.

In new avenues, creativity and innovative methodologies are slowing gaining acceptance. As an example, I had the opportunity to assist with an agile implementation process in one of Spain's major banks. There was a team of agile coaches, and each member was assigned to a different division of the bank. They were tasked with studying how their respective divisions were benefiting from the implementation of agile.

The bank's senior management made a clear commitment to the adoption of agile as a way to streamline, lighten, and improve the organization's overall operations. Despite having an internal team of agile coaches, they were having difficulty expanding and implementing agile in the different departments. The bank operated under typical vertical departmental structures, and there was a tendency for people in the command line to resist or even ignore recommendations. Senior management saw LSP as a way to more amicably penetrate those areas where reluctance to accept agile was impeding the process. And they were correct. The results and conclusions of the LSP dynamic helped the coaches to pursue implementing agile throughout the bank with far greater success.

LSP CHALLENGES

A few years ago, I had the opportunity to introduce LSP to the principal and director of a Catholic school. This man was also a practicing priest. Because the Catholic church has strict beliefs in certain absolute truths, it would be easy to assume this was not a situation that would be welcoming to a methodology that seeks a variety of solutions.

For added context, it is necessary to understand the state of education in Spain. It is one of those fields in which it is extremely difficult to innovate. The study plans and curricula are extremely rigid, and any attempt to improve education from a creative and participatory point of view usually clashes with the strict structure. At most, there may be small aesthetic changes. But the country's curriculum is significantly out-of-date.

In addition to its rigidity, Spain's educational system expects youth to make decisions for which the average adolescent is not prepared. At the age of 14, students must begin to choose a course of study with minimal guidance and preparation; and these decisions will carry over into university. Family, friends, and tradition will influence their decisions. In effect, these youth must set their life path without the knowledge and experience to make an informed decision, while dealing with pressures from others who would choose this for them.

Because it is very difficult to modify learning and curricular models, I decided working with the school would be a good opportunity to apply LSP in the field of academic and professional guidance. I wanted to use this methodology to help the youth learn to make better choices for their own futures. I ran a series of workshops in which I challenged the students with different introspective exercises. Through these, they could dictate or reinforce their true motivations, objectives and, ultimately, what they wanted to do with their academic and professional futures.

I have observed a variety of factors that can create bias when making decisions. So I purposely designed my workshops to isolate these influences:

- Family members and tradition: Relatives will want their youth to follow the family path. If a grandfather was a doctor, and one of the youth's parents is a doctor, it is normal practice for the child to follow this path and study medicine.
- The social environment: If the majority of the student's good friends are pursuing one academic line, there is a good chance the student will follow along and choose the same.
- A teenage crush: When a teen develops an attraction toward another, they may likely consider following the same path as their crush.
- The digital environment and social influencers: These can expose youth to an unrealistic way of life. While inaccurate, the youth do not understand this and may allow it to influence them as they make important decisions.
- The academic environment: Well-intentioned members of the student's educational community, such as teachers and tutors, will try to help the student choose their direction.

At the end of the day, the students will be the ones to bear the consequences of a right or wrong decision. They are the ones who will be going on to deal with the university path they chose at such a premature stage. And after university, they are the ones who will be fighting to have a successful career that is a continuation of all their hard work in school.

One's academic career involves a significant investment of money, time, and study. This is why, when presented with the opportunity to work with adolescents,

I felt it so important to provide them with access to tools like LEGO® SERIOUS PLAY®. LSP could deliberately remove the influences from these students, allowing them to discover their authentic selves and thereby the course of studies and vocational options best suited to them.

I have had the opportunity to run many workshops using the LSP methodology. One aspect that always catches my attention is the high percentage of people who simply do not feel any passion for their jobs. They are well-educated and have good skills and a high degree of knowledge, but they feel like they are in the wrong place. They had to make a decision about their lives at a young age, but they did not make the right choices for themselves. As a result, they grew into unmotivated workers lacking passion. Their careers are nothing more to them than a necessity for economic support. How different would society be if people had more opportunities to explore themselves, evaluate themselves, and somehow take complete control of their own destinies?

Weeks after I held that first series of workshops with the students, the school principal called me. He wanted to let me know how pleased their parents were. They could see the satisfaction in their children's faces as they talked about the experience of having worked on their own development while simply using a few Lego® bricks. Many of these parents commented on their frustration at not being able to help their children make the best possible decision. They were pleasantly surprised when they discovered the students just needed the appropriate atmosphere to let them be themselves, while beginning to mature and become aware of the relevance of their own decisions in regard to their future.

▬ LSP AND TECHNOLOGY ▬▬▬▬▬▬▬▬▬▬▬▬▬▬▬▬▬▬▬▬▬

Now let us consider how LSP can be utilized in the pursuit of digital transformation. I am a regular collaborator with a private university, which has a presence in the main cities of the country. In Spain, two models of higher education coexist: public state education and private. Each model has its good sides and bad sides, but they coexist in harmony while offering an important range of options to the national and international student community.

It is curious to observe how universities remain, in some aspects, obsolete and anchored to past roles and positions. People think of universities as being avant-garde, spearheading countless projects, studies and advances for society. Yet it is curious to observe how, in many regards, they remain obsolete and anchored to past roles and positions. A clear example of this would be digital transformation.

While it seems a fact many of their processes should by now be digitized, many universities still lack even minimally digitized systems and procedures.

The COVID-19 pandemic forced universities to deal with their suboptimal digitization efforts. No longer being able to teach face-to-face, they were obligated to find new methods to continue educating. This has accelerated their digitization to what some studies indicate is a five-year breakthrough in the span of just a few months. I had the opportunity to see this for myself, while using LSP to assist Valencia University in the digitization of internal processes.

I observed many of these changes from analog to digital do not have so much to do with availability of technological solutions, but rather with people. In general, humans see change as a threat and therefore are not predisposed to welcome that which is new and different. As such, forced change processes are doomed to failure. This is why LSP was the perfect tool to help with the institution's digitization implementation. It is far easier for people to change their minds when they are the ones to visualize a new process and convince themselves it is necessary. Through different LSP workshops, we were able to help participants understand the need to incorporate a series of new habits and customs in their day-to-day work. We focused on showing how technology could be a valuable ally rather than a threat.

In my work, I have learned just how much people and organizations can benefit, grow, and adapt when they are willing to take the risk of embracing creative and innovative tools like LEGO® SERIOUS PLAY®. We should not allow outdated beliefs to hinder progress or ultimately prevent a better well-being for all. Benjamin Franklin said there are three types of people: those who are immovable, those who are movable, and those who move. Many years later, Sir Ken Robinson added to this by saying we need to encourage people from the last group to move. Once they do, the result will become, in the best sense of the word, a revolution. And this is what we need.

10

USA: BREAKING THROUGH THE FEAR OF FAILURE

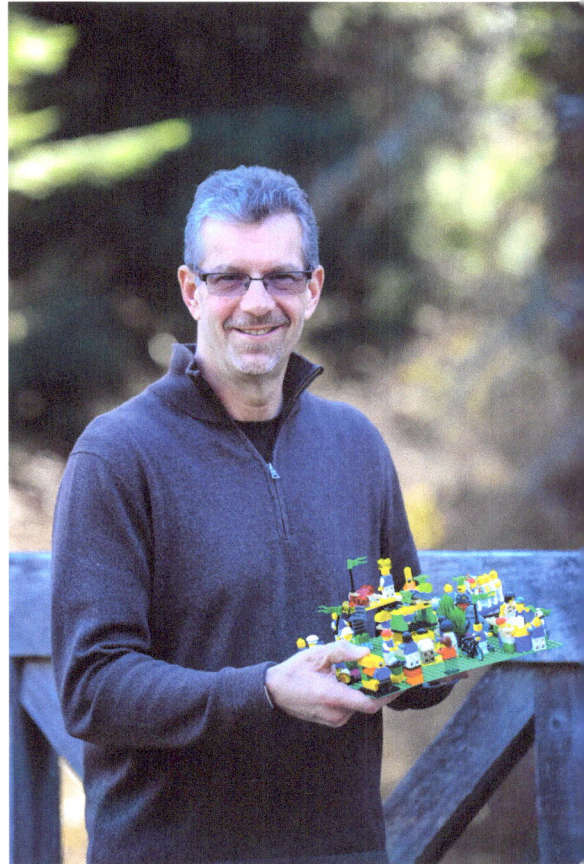

By Greg Bliss

The culture of the United States is unique. When deploying LEGO® SERIOUS PLAY® methods, there are aspects of American culture manifesting themselves in ways that pose facilitation challenges. I have frequently encountered cultural resisters, and I have developed ways to facilitate and frame LSP to bring participants into a place where they can fully engage in effective creative problem-solving and innovative thinking. I am going to share how to:

- Help participants stay in the optimal learner's mindset.
- Nurture psychological safety so participants can ease into being authentic and vulnerable, sharing their unique perspectives.
- Level the playing field so everyone offers their expertise without coming off as too forward, directive, or domineering.
- Slow down the American bias for action, using LSP to create more complete and robust solutions rather than jumping from ideas to implementation.

▬▬ GETTING THE BEST FROM EVERYONE ▬▬▬▬▬▬▬▬

My passion is to help individuals, teams, and organizations thrive. The drive to help others get the best from themselves and others comes from nine years working within corporate America. First, I was a marketer for Herman Miller; and then I was an Advertising Executive at Leo Burnett. Both are great companies; but in each instance, some of the unique skills I had remained dormant. And that is how I created my company's mission: How to help you show up in a way that you can be your authentic self and use all of your skills.

My business focuses on three areas:

- Driving organizational change—Creating a vision, strategic direction, and culture to support the desired destination. I also enable the organization to build the needed skills and partnerships to thrive.
- Developing leaders—All change initiatives need leaders to be very present and to mentor/model where the company needs to go. I coach executive level talent, mid-level managers, and first-time supervisors.
- Facilitating creativity and innovation—Exploring new and novel ways to address challenges and opportunities.

I have always been an experiential facilitator, injecting my background of improvisation (Second City), TV presenter, radio announcer, and theatrical actor into the designs of highly engaging, interactive environments. Activities and hands-on learning allow me to introduce unique tools that give more meaning to new content and allow participants to decide how to integrate new ideas into their current thinking.

I knew LSP would become a primary tool for me as soon as I discovered it. Ten years ago, I met Jacquie Lloyd Smith at the annual Creative Problem Solving Institute (CPSI) conference in Buffalo. Jacquie was conducting a one-day preconference workshop entitled Introduction to LSP. I was a blank slate. My only LEGO® experience was building with the bricks in my youth. Jacquie turned on a light bulb for me that day. The LSP methodology was such a powerful way to create 100% engagement, uncover deep insights by thinking with my hands, and create and tell stories using 3D models. I instantly knew this method had to be in my tool kit.

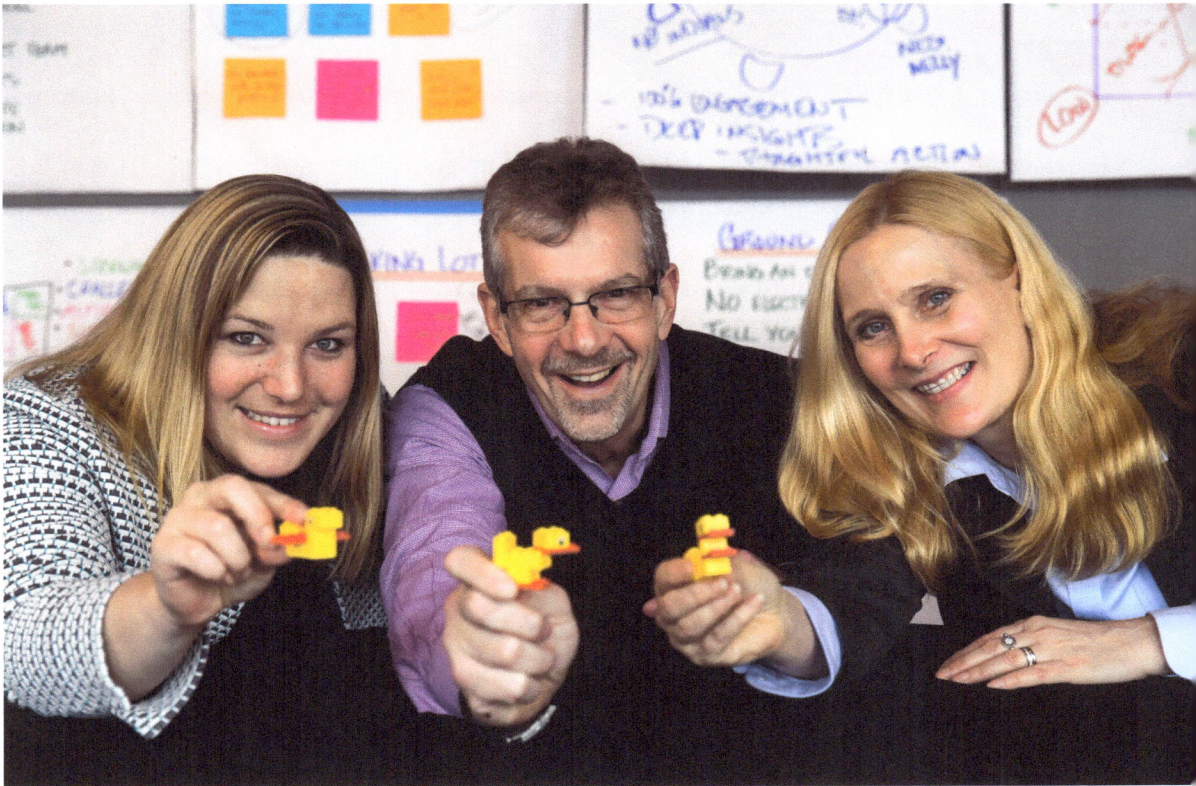

Immediately after CPSI, I built what I believed to be a very powerful LSP program using the foundational builds from Jacquie's session. I was thoroughly convinced this was a robust program ready to roll out. After creating a PowerPoint presentation to support my new learning, I sent the deck to Jacquie to confirm I had listened well and was ready to sell LSP to clients.

The next day, my phone rang. It was Jacquie calling with some feedback regarding my program. She was both kind and clear. Yes, I had listened well. But no, these introductory builds did not make a full program. In fact, the one-day introduction I attended was but "the little pink spoon," a taste of how LSP could be applied. There were whole worlds of LSP I had not seen. Jacquie invited me to Whistler to participate in Strategic Play's Teams and Groups program, which was my first certification in LEGO® SERIOUS PLAY®. The rest is LSP history.

I have now acquired six Strategic Play certifications, which I have integrated into my work with all kinds of organizations. These include Fortune 100 companies, mid-size firms, and new start-ups. I have also taught workshops and mentored new businesses at 1871, the largest business incubator in the country.

FEAR OF FAILURE

No one likes doing things where they feel inferior. This is especially true in U.S. organizations. Leaders are often expected to possess knowledge of methods and the expertise necessary to apply them. When a toddler learns to walk, they first wobble, fall, tenuously balance, take a few tentative steps, amble, and then finally learn to run. Leaders in the U.S. think of themselves as born runners, right from the get-go.

This fear of not looking good inhibits building the necessary foundational and facilitation skills needed to deliver LSP in a number of ways:

- Leaders remain in their perceived safe zone and rarely, if ever, venture out into the learning zone. They are rarely in flow.
- They protect themselves from making the mistakes that are the crucial learning moments to build skills.
- These participants mistake *knowing* the content for being able to facilitate that content.
- They leave the course with a diminished tool kit and fail to integrate LSP concepts into their future facilitation engagements.

How do I know when someone is protecting themselves and their self-image? Usually, these people will criticize their own 3D models. They think they are not good builders. They may constantly redo their build, hoping to make it good enough.

From a facilitator's perspective, I am able to quiet their inner-critic by doing the following:

- Explaining that it is not about the quality of the model. The important part is telling a rich and transparent story that has emotional context.
- Being non-evaluative about all the builds, stories, and potential actions. Each has an equal value. All the information they share is useful.
- Bringing laughter into the training room. I usually make a mistake early in the course and then laugh at myself. This helps to emphasize the importance of being present, rather than perfect, throughout the training. Demonstrating my willingness to be vulnerable permits them to do the same. Their hard shells crack and they emerge as being engaged without any airs or pretenses.

BEAT THE CLOCK

I conducted my first training for certifying facilitators in LSP methods along with Stephen Walling of Strategic Play. One participant, who had a master's degree in creativity and many other educational accomplishments, was there to assimilate the information so they could use it in a training the following week. My Spidey sense—yes, my LEGO® Superhero is Spiderman— started to tingle.

After every exercise or build, this person immediately began asking a slew of rapid-fire questions about how and when you would use that build. Clearly, two things were going on. First, they were in a get-the-answers mode, rather than simply relaxing into being a participant. And second, they were under extreme pressure to design and employ LSP coming from ground zero.

I see this beat-the-clock, just give me the answers mentality often enough to have a story ready that defuses the tension:

I was on vacation in Sonoma Valley, doing some wine tasting. One of the smaller craft wineries was cut into the side of a hill. As I entered the cave, I saw three kinds of fermenting vessels: Oak barrels, ceramic casks, and aluminum vats.

As I tasted some vintages, I asked the wine maker about what I assumed were the three separate wines he was fermenting. He corrected me by saying, "These three kinds of containers all hold the same wine. I know what I want it to taste like at the end of the fermentation process. So I taste the wine from each container, and then 'blend at the end' the perfect character I'm striving for."

This is what I tell participants: Take the time to be an LSP learner first. not a deliverer. Stay in a learner's mindset the entire three days. Then blend what you have learned into what you what already know and want to do at the end. I find participants respond well to that story. At the conclusion of the training, they are grateful they did not constantly try to apply their learning prematurely.

BE AMAZING DAILY

The practice of pretending everything is great or fantastic, even when it is not, is pervasive in American culture. Ask most people how they are doing, and you routinely hear, "Couldn't be better," or "Living the dream." I am guilty of this myself. We all are, to some extent.

When we cannot say what is wrong or admit to not knowing something, we do it to prevent showing weakness or being vulnerable. We are self-protective by nature. The very thing that will accelerate our learning and growth is these disclosures we cannot make to ourselves or others. The pressure to constantly be amazing is intense. It is hard. And it gets in the way of acquiring new skills and knowledge.

Psychological safety is the antidote. The concept is imbedded within the LSP methodology. Google's landmark Aristotle study, around how to build the perfect high-functioning team, amplified the importance of psychological safety.

During a particular training, a participant disclosed some very personal information. We had only been in the workshop for an hour on day one, when they chose to share they had lost their job, their marriage was in trouble, they had moved in with a new companion, and their child was acting out. Phew.

And this illustrates the power of LSP: Everyone in attendance thought over what the individual revealed; and before I could say anything, the participants:

- Affirmed this person.
- Thanked them for trusting the group with their disclosures.
- Told the person they were there for them.

Not only did this individual feel psychologically safe enough to share their personal challenges, but the group was equally able to hear, accept, and affirm where this person was.

I have seen LSP create this safe learning environment time and time again. In fact, I have never seen it fail to create the rich and collaborative climate for model building and storytelling. As a facilitator, enabling psychological safety happens when you:

- Make yourself equally available to everyone, without playing favorites.
- Democratize storytelling air time.
- Weave collaborative challenges into your program design.
- Value all ideas, stories, and concepts equally.
- Take the participants on a collective journey of discovery.

It no longer matters whether we are perfect and have all the answers. The group and the methodology will cocreate everything we need to find.

More than any other method I have used, LSP engenders psychological safety. It melts away the perfect mask we project to conceal our true self; and instead, it takes us on a journey of enlightenment.

STUMP THE TRAINER

This baiting of the facilitator happens during almost every certification training. It also occurs wherever a community of practice gets together, such as Creative Problem Solving Institute (CPSI). At the start of the training or during a break, someone will come up to me and ask a question on a topic of which they are the expert. The motivation seems to be they have deep skills too and need to prove it. I will not play that game.

One of the cornerstones of all experiential training is we leverage the collective wisdom of the group. Instead of playing Stump the Trainer, I turn that into Who Has Some Insight? LSP is a rich platform for the expert contributions of *all* the participants. We can share our expertise and align our stories through the creation of a shared model. This allows us to tell a very powerful story to the larger organization.

I recently worked with an automotive parts manufacturer that has plants in North and South America. They needed to roll out a new set of organizational competencies. We began by putting employees into groups of seven, because there were seven different competencies. Each person was assigned one competency. And ZAP, they were each expected to be the expert on that particular competency and answer the following questions:

- What is the scope of this competency?
- What are the key behaviors associated with it?
- How might this competency benefit the organization?

Once employees had some ideas around each of these questions, out came LSP. Following some foundational skill building, we asked these executives to build a 3D model of their competency, including the key behaviors. After each of these experts had built and taken turns sharing their models (teaching their peers), we then asked each group to arrange the models to create a powerful narrative arc:

1 Telling a repeatable, engaging story for others.
2 Enabling the entire organization to have a shared understanding of these competencies.

We cascaded this exercise all the way down to the plant floor in all locations. LSP turned everyone into an expert about information they previously had no connection to.

BIAS FOR ACTION

U.S. leaders tend to tell others what they think everyone else should do. They see challenges or opportunities and immediately direct the action. Culturally, leaders are programmed to have the answers and to implement solutions in real time. Being in motion is good—we are doing something. Reflecting first and contemplating all the facets of the presenting problem is viewed as neutral or bad—nothing tangible is happening.

The blind spot for action-first leaders is there is seldom a robust solution to put in motion. Most times, there are pitfalls, gaps, traps, and false assumptions that necessitate new thinking and revising the current solution. That burns time, man-hours, and resources.

Drivers can utilize LSP to:

- More clearly define the current situation, root causes of the problem, and crystalize a cogent challenge question.
- Generate deep insights that can be combined into a set of high-potential actions.
- Build out all the elements of the solution. This tends to be the largest blind spot for leaders: Do the due diligence to flesh out all the contingencies.
- Create an action plan for implementation and capturing feedback.

■■■ MY FINAL THOUGHTS ■■■

LSP is a powerful method for enabling 100% engagement, uncovering deep insights that lead to thought action.

To turbocharge the learning of the organizations you work with, remember to:

- Keep participants in a learner's mindset throughout the training. Give them permission to blend at the end, to solidify their new learning and its possible applications.
- Nurture psychological safety so people let go of the urge to be amazing. Doing so will allow the group's collective wisdom to come into play.
- Democratize the "experts." Turn them from proving their smarts to the facilitator towards sharing their insightful stories with the group. Allow them to play in the group, rather than to set themselves above and apart from others.
- Make participants aware of all the steps in the creative problem-solving process. Going from ideas straight to execution will save them from many pitfalls and time-eating rework.

Having this perspective on U.S. clients will allow you maximize the value of LSP and take them from good to great.

11

CONCLUSION

We wrote this book to provide you, the reader, with a selection of reflections and short stories from our work with LEGO® SERIOUS PLAY® methods around the world. Just as the world is diverse, so are our experiences. We each contributed our experiences to help you understand the power of the LSP process as we have witnessed it in our work. We have helped people around the globe improve how they communicate so they can better understand each other, while finding better outcomes and solutions to pressing challenges.

The LEGO SERIOUS PLAY method ultimately helps everyone to clearly express their ideas as they tell better stories, aided by the visuals of their 3D models. Being able to see what others are saying and thinking helps participants to listen at deeper levels and gain a better understanding of others' perspectives. Through this process, they are better able to gather key information they can then use as they collaborate to solve problems. This helps participants to produce results they would not have been able to attain without the aid of such an innovative application.

We opened with a reflection from Jesper, in Denmark, explaining how they tested the LEGO® SERIOUS PLAY® method during its early days at the LEGO Systems Group. He shared how it all began, where it is today, and where it might take us as we move into the future.

From there, the book moved through the countries in alphabetical order. This was our attempt to clearly identify that no one country or location is superior to another. Each country represented here has its own unique and interesting story worth telling regarding the reach of the LSP method.

Dabs took the reader on a short visit to the vast continent of Africa, specifically Nigeria. He described Africa as the last frontier, rich in so many natural resources. It is also known as the continent with the largest number of young people in the world. Dabs showed us how this continent has grown in creativity despite its enormous lack of resources. He highlighted how LEGO® SERIOUS PLAY® methods have and are proving to be useful in unlocking the continent's huge untapped potential.

We then moved our focus to Brazil, where Kari, Ivonne, and Paulo painted a colorful picture of the creative and fun-loving Brazilian culture where personal relationships are key in all business transactions. They described the benefits and pitfalls of a culture that embodies a style of overexplaining and indecisiveness, which can slow down the process of doing business while causing frustration. They also highlighted how LEGO SERIOUS PLAY methods have been instrumental in assisting to alter communication styles, helping people to articulate their meaning clearly and effectively.

Our next stop was with Jacquie in Canada. She showed us how she introduced LEGO SERIOUS PLAY and its value to the country from what appeared to be an unlikely starting place: Thunder Bay, Ontario. This Northern Ontario locale created an incubator for success, allowing LSP methods to spread through the region and eventually reaching coast to coast. Despite the generally conservative and risk-averse attitudes of Canadians, LSP proved hugely successful because it allows people to have objective conversations while ensuring everyone gets to share their story.

We then moved east to China, where Brian told the story of a common perception of global vs. local amongst the people of mainland China, Macau, and Hong Kong. People infer a sense of credibility when they hear about international and well-known brands such as LEGO®. This shows the importance of featuring both international and local adoption of such an innovative methodology. He also described the position of the teacher/instructor, who is viewed as the expert in the classroom, and how he has worked to create a level playing field while facilitating LEGO SERIOUS PLAY.

Next, we visited Germany. Sven explained how regional stereotypes can be helpful in understanding the subtle differences between people. He highlighted the existence of these clichés exist and how they can characterize a culture to a certain extent. He further explained that in the context of business challenges, issues that present on the surface are often only the outer shell of a problem. Sven used a case study to illustrates how useful LSP can be when it comes to identifying the true core of a challenging situation.

Then the story moved us into the boardrooms of Mexico with Hugo, where he has been using play to bring forward extraordinary results in a business culture that loves to discuss and talk but is slow when it comes to making decisions. He has used LEGO® SERIOUS PLAY® methods to successfully help teams visualize their big picture, create new ideas, and integrate different perspectives to create creative strategies. Hugo has applied LSP to build trust among team members, which is a necessary for teams to function and excel.

Rosa, who lives in Panama City, highlighted how LEGO SERIOUS PLAY methods are being increasingly accepted by the country's younger population of users. These individuals want more out life than the traditional path of earlier generations, so they seek careers that are both fun and fulfilling. Rosa explained how she brought LSP to Panama and Central America as the methodology was just starting to gain momentum. She also shared how she has used the tool with not just businesses, but also with some of Panama's elite athletes.

We then landed in Spain, where Arturo described some of the country's history and the range of diversity amongst its inhabitants. He also examined the traditional lens through which the people of Spain view creativity. The country is rich in imagination, but it is relegated to the most traditional venues such as dance and the visual arts. Arturo showed how, through his work, he has observed a nontraditional view of creativity slowly taking hold and growing throughout the country. He has utilized LSP in banking and educational settings, amongst others. Seeing the shifting attitude keeps Arturo motivated in his quest to help the people in his region appreciate a wider scope of the concept of creativity.

Our last chapter took us into corporate world of the United States of America, where Greg explained aspects of American culture that can manifest in ways that pose facilitation issues. Greg identified three key challenges in his chapter and showed how LEGO SERIOUS PLAY methods have been instrumental in dealing with each. Specifically, he explained how LSP slows down the process of thinking and reinforces the learner's mindset. It creates psychological safety so the new group's collective wisdom can emerge. Because everyone's story gets equal airtime, it democratizes the experts and allows the entire group to contribute to the collective story while crafting new solutions.

We are humbly aware we are not experts, and it took a considerable amount of courage from each of us to share our experiences with you. Simply put, we are practitioners with stories we felt were interesting enough to share. We truly hope our stories will provide insight or create space for you to reflect on your personal stories as well. We realize everyone has their own narrative and that each is different, and this is what makes us unique.

While this book has come to its conclusion, the story is in a perpetual state of creation. We are well aware that so many new stories are emerging from the global playground. As we seek to hear and include everyone's story and voice, we would love to hear from you too. If you have just read this book but never used LEGO® SERIOUS PLAY®, you have only just begun what will prove to be an amazing journey into the power of play. We strongly encourage you to sign up and take the certification training we are offering globally and also online. You will uncover your own unique stories and those of the people around you. While this book is only available in English, we offer LEGO SERIOUS PLAY methods training in several different languages.

If you are already an LSP practitioner and you want to contribute to this collection, please write to us with your story. We would love to hear how you are using this method in your corner of the world. We also want to thank all the participants who have trusted us enough to pick up the bricks, to build something unique, and to share their wonderful stories with us.

Finally, we want to thank you for joining us on our reflective global journey. We can't wait to hear your story!

www.ingramcontent.com/pod-product-compliance
Lightning Source LLC
Chambersburg PA
CBHW041950220326
41599CB00004BA/150